SIGNS OF LIFE

SIGNS OF LIFE

ALFRED APPEL, JR.

ALFRED A. KNOPF   NEW YORK   1983

THIS IS A BORZOI BOOK
PUBLISHED BY ALFRED A. KNOPF, INC.

Library of Congress Cataloging in Publication Data
Appel, Alfred. Signs of life.
1. Photography, Artistic. I. Title.
TR642.A66 1983   770   83-47960
ISBN 0-394-50773-8

Manufactured in the United States of America
First Edition

FRONTISPIECE: Edward Weston, *Outdoor lot, M-G-M Studios, Culver City, California, 1939*. The side-wheeler "Maria Theresa," on the right, is from *The Great Waltz* (1938), and is real, as are the small boats in the rear, which are "beached" before a painted flat of the Marseilles waterfront that was used in *Port of Seven Seas* (1938).

To Nina, Karen, and Richard

Contents

SIGNS OF LIFE

Russell Lee, *In Front of a Movie Theatre, Chicago, April 1941*.

Coming Attractions

Coming Attractions

This book aspires to read and understand photographs and the basis of their appeal. The images will be seen at once as aesthetic objects, gems of their kind, and constituents of a larger visual culture—"reel life," mainly, as Joyce termed the movies in *Finnegans Wake,* which was published in 1939, when motion pictures were taken more seriously than they are now as a constant source of inspiration and instruction. The pun on "reel" was already old when Joyce first used it, but it still has some life in it, particularly if you're able to identify a specific child star on TV as the source of your young son's or nephew's manner of speech and swagger. As a linguistic model, the first-rate pun or portmanteau word represents a gnomic, associative ideal: the idea of the truth compressed in a very small space. The prose pieces in this book, which blend formalist analysis, cultural history, and memoir, hope to do no less. Television will be treated rudely near the end, without "pudding the carp before doevre hors" (Joyce). There will be singing and dancing early on, and pictures of beautiful men and women will appear at midpoint, just when they are needed. Literature, photography, and cinema will commingle as equals, and no apologies will be tendered. Nor will the proprieties of photography criticism be allowed to inhibit the readings. Tags such as "realist" and "symbolist," often used to describe the opposite poles of image-making, will prove less helpful here.

The photographs by two realists, Russell Lee (left) and Tod Papageorge (p. 7), suggest how the connotative richness of a strong quotidian image will lift it beyond its category in the pages ahead, particularly if the viewer narrows the psychic distance between himself and the picture. This narrowing activity is the central reflexive action of this book, whose author was born in 1934. This bold fact is introduced here to justify 1941 as a starting point; a year held firmly in mind is a context for pictures of every kind (history should rhyme and scan, especially one's own). Russell Lee's photo was taken in Chicago, in 1941, of course, for the Farm Security Administration, and demonstrates unambiguously that ladies and gentlemen used to wear their Sunday best to the picture show. This is telescoped by the brand-new shoes in the foreground, whose owner is playing to the street as well as to the photographer (his gaze to the right enlarges the picture). Movies and moviegoing constitute a definite plus in these lives. A gestalt psychologist might claim that the graphic whirlpool around "Plus" draws the viewer toward the scene, bringing one closer to the imaginative and self-confident fel-

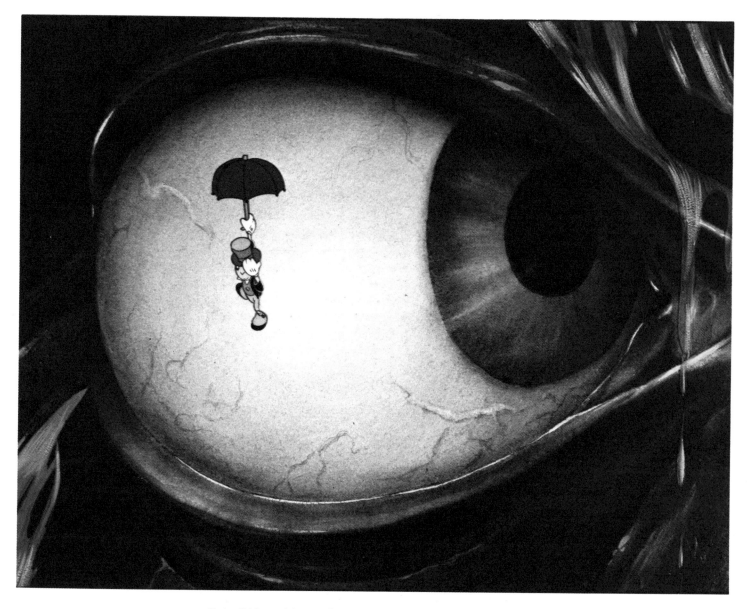

Jiminy Cricket and the eye of Monstro the whale. © Walt Disney Productions.

low at center stage. His poised and grounded "walking stick," the symbolic center of the image, ought to pull one into the scene completely. Too thin to be a bona fide store-bought cane, the "walking stick" is probably a former curtain rod or schoolroom pointer, improvised to complete some fantasy of ideal form and essence. On "the playground of the mind" (Huizinga's phrase), this strip of wood or metal is a swank's walking stick (Adolphe Menjou in the movies), a song-and-dance man's prop, a hepcat bandleader's jive baton, a dreamer's scepter or wand. We've been in his shoes.

If these scepters and proverbial shoes seem too arbitrary and privileged to be apt, then the doubloon chapter of *Moby-Dick* (1851) should be read, reread, or remembered. The doubloon is a gold coin from Ecuador which Captain Ahab has nailed to the main mast of the *Pequod* as a prize for the crew member who first sights the white whale. Each of the book's principal characters meditates aloud on the coin's ambiguous symbolism, each seeing something different, "mirror[ing] back his own mysterious self," as Ahab says. Even the significance of the date of this photograph, 1941, a full and famous year in American history, is up for grabs on one of the *Pequod*'s smaller masts.

A middle-aged American eye (and mind) trained on 1941 remembers that, around this time, age six or seven, he saw his first feature-length film, *Pinocchio,* the year's worst trauma. By critical consensus Disney's masterpiece, it survives today as more than one viewer-victim's measuring stick for subsequent states of movie- or life-induced panic and terror. Its happy ending was missed by some 1940–41 movie tyros whose heads were buried under their coats—and, later, bedclothes—since well-educated, progressive mothers tried to challenge and overcome such fearfulness in their children by reading them the original book. In fact, the book was even scarier (there were no various movie spin-off books whose illustrations would have preserved the many reassuring if sentimental aspects of the film, especially the sight of Geppetto's shop window glowing at night, golden-hued like Rembrandt, an image of one's own room as safe harbor). After the light was turned off, a child in the wake of *Pinocchio* insisted on having his door left ajar, and prayed that he wouldn't have another nightmare in which he was chased and swallowed by Monstro the whale, caged by Stromboli, or transformed in one way or another. Then the child would try to sleep with one eye open and fixed on the window, especially on stormy nights, when criminals and Nazi spies were more likely to be out on the prowl. Most of the time, however, an average boy of the late nineteen-thirties and World War II years felt surprisingly secure, tucked in as he was each night below a splendid illustrated wall map or a color photo of General MacArthur, firm jaw to the wind, the American flag streaming behind him. Jiminy Cricket might well have alighted on one's night table, shaken the ocean water off his frame, and sung a rousing patriotic song as he twirled his furled umbrella, his parachute-scepter. A child of the period could remember the rule of only one Mayor of New York

Dick Tracy and Pat Patton, 1941, in pursuit of
Krome, a murderer. © 1941 Chicago Tribune–
New York News Syndicate, Inc.

City (1933–45), one President of the United States (1933–45), one Pope of Rome (1939–58), and one Heavyweight Champion of the World (1937–49).

The twentieth century would catch up with these children, in one way or another, and so would Monstro—the reality of one's final reel. Where's the wand or scepter, or even the walking stick? It wouldn't hurt anyone to have a secular icon to take the place of General MacArthur. Tod Papageorge's 1976 Bicentennial view of Coast Guard cutters in their Fourth of July berths during Operation Sail is just such an image (right). This place, and formally composed space, is an ideal port of debarkation and re-entry, a conjunction of technological clutter and a chaotic urban plenitude that, on closer examination, turns out to be supremely ordered and festive, animated as it is by a deceptively large group of visitors, a hide-and-seek presence, a challenge (Find the Adult Who's Regained his Scepter and is Pretending he's Captain), and graced above all by an electronic halo on top of the central mast. God is a radio beam, to adapt what Stephen Dedalus says in *Ulysses* (1922) about a child's "shout in the street." If other viewers see the picture this way, too, they may wish to clip it out of their extra study copy. Then trace the masts, gun barrels, and various oblique lines on a sheet of thin white paper and you'll have a close-up of winter grass on fresh snow, and a sense of how the picture's formal structure is governed by the play of numberless verticals, a game of picked-up sticks, a phrase which describes the course of this book. Then tack the photo to the wall by the bed, where it can serve as an icon, aesthetic object, or trompe l'oeil window or porthole; the need, the rage for order and security and beauty is hardly unique. *Cut along dotted line,* as it used to say on cardboard ship models and paper dolls of Ann Sheridan or Ann Sothern as a WAC or nurse. Now turn on the portable TV set, in the hope of finding a star-spangled movie from 1941–42 that would provide a partial index of the life of the period, a context for pictures, and a "trip down Memory Lane," to quote a limp squib in this week's *TV Prevues,* which was written by yet another fellow who's lost his walking stick and scepter.

Tod Papageorge, *New York City, July 5, 1976.*

HOLLYWOOD MEETS PHOTOGRAPHY

James Cagney in *Yankee Doodle Dandy,* 1942.

"Over there! Over there!" sang the three eight-year-old boys as they strutted out the side exit doors of the Playhouse Theatre (its actual name). Turning right, toward home, they danced and skipped down the middle of the tree-lined street in this Long Island town, leaping across and skirting the sun-stippled shadows of elms and maples, as though these were the chalked guidelines of some codified street or sidewalk game. It was the Fourth of July, 1942, the first Independence Day of World War II. The flags and banners were all up, there had been a compact yet splendid parade at 10:00 A.M., and the boys had just seen *Yankee Doodle Dandy,* starring James Cagney as George M. Cohan, composer of "You're a Grand Old Flag" (the film's finale, pictured on the left) and "Over There," the place where modern American wars are fought. If the Coast Guard patrol blimp that regularly went in search of enemy subs had circled back and photographed this town from above on any afternoon save Saturdays, the enlarged prints would have revealed the state of mind of young America: tiny movie-inspired Marines and soldiers on battle maneuvers in the woods and marshes off Long Island Sound, readying themselves for America's first offensive campaign of the war, the amphibious invasion of—no one knew where, yet. But one month later, August 7, 1942, eight months after the Japanese attack on Pearl Harbor, the secret target turned out to be Guadalcanal, a difficult place to find on the map. One waited impatiently for *Life* magazine and newsreels and feature-length motion picture fictions to see what *over there* really looked like.

The American flag appeared everywhere. Magazines featured it on their covers, from the outré patriotism of *Vogue* to the no-nonsense approach of *Life* and *Look.* Starlets and comic-book superheroes such as Captain America and Wonder Woman wore it as unselfconsciously as Uncle Sam, or at least the stalwart Uncle Sam pictured on posters rather than the rumpled one played by Walter Huston in *Yankee Doodle Dandy*'s show-within-a-show. Donald Duck wore it as pajamas in a patriotic animated short, and it seemed to wave from the upper right-hand corner of a *Don Winslow of the Navy* Big Little Book when its pages were quickly flipped. Children saluted it whenever they could, pledged allegiance to it at school each day, drew it in art class, and accepted low grades for taking excessive liberties with its design and colors. Assumptions about "national purpose," as it is called now, were shared by one and all. Hollywood and the editors of mass magazines agreed with the government that death should be ignored or minimized. *Pride of the Yankees* (1942), a movie about the life and tragic early death of the great baseball player, Lou Gehrig, ended with his 1939 farewell speech to the fans at flag-bedecked Yankee Stadium, omitting altogether the final two years of his decline. He wasn't shown on his deathbed until after the war, in *The Babe Ruth Story* (1948). *Life* didn't picture American corpses until 1943, when it printed George Strock's 1942 photograph of three dead soldiers lying face-down on Buna Beach, New Guinea, the back of the foreground corpse covered with maggots (p. 13). The public was shocked as well as surprised, enlistments dropped the following week, and the editors vowed not to publish such a demoralizing picture again.

The impact and history of George Strock's Buna Beach picture impart the authority if not the supremacy of photographic images. Although the War Department's censors never objected to *Life*'s vivid written accounts of deadly jungle war, they did delay by seven months the publication of the Buna photograph (Strock's censored picture-story led off the issue of February 15, 1943). Nor were there any complaints when the magazine published grotesque photos of charred Japanese bodies and dismembered heads, their teeth hideous in death, an extension of the dehumanizing racist caricatures found everywhere in the visual culture. There was no such direct preparation for Buna Beach, not even by way of some pictorial evidence of singed Caucasian German corpses. When *Life* finally printed the withheld Buna photo, the editors paired it with an incantatory full-page editorial titled "Three Americans" (September 20, 1943). A burst of gunfire had killed the men, "apparently not from the barge, but from a machine-gun nest located in the direction of where you, the readers, are sitting," explained *Life,* trying to draw each reader-viewer into the picture, in this case for his own good (retrospective opinions about the basic intentions of photojournalism and old Hollywood are more mixed than this). "And the reason we print [the photo] now," the editorial states, "is that, last week, President Roosevelt and Elmer Davis [director, Office of War Information] and the War Department decided that the American people ought to

be able to see their own boys as they fell in battle; to come directly and without words into the presence of their own dead. And so here it is. This is the reality that lies behind the names that come to rest at last in monuments in the leafy squares of busy American towns." *Life*'s explanatory words didn't matter. Reality over there was overpowering, and unwelcome, though it could be considered obliquely, as in the celebrated case of Flattop, an amusing 1943–44 villain in *Dick Tracy,* who drowned in a city park lagoon around the time of D-Day when his jacket caught on a piling which looked like an enemy anti-invasion obstacle at high tide. Letters of condolence poured in to his creator, Chester Gould, as though a name had been affixed to one of the unidentified dead boys of Buna Beach.

The photograph in question, if not the taboo subject, has become as familiar to perusers of Time-Life anthologies as the still from *Yankee Doodle Dandy,* whose point of view implies an unimpeded view from the best seat in the house, where no detail should escape notice. Note the way the Captain of the smokestack has the bridge almost to himself in Papageorge's photo (p. 7), the best command assignment he's had since he was seven years old, when he had in fantasy projected himself on *Life* magazine's version of the great new battleship U.S.S. *North Carolina.* The Buna photo has now been reprinted in at least six Time-Life picture books, five of them published between 1973 and 1979, by which time the intensity and verisimilitude of television and motion picture violence had inured most spectators to the

George Strock, *Dead American soldiers, Buna Beach, 1942.* © 1943 Time, Inc.

Above: Weegee, ca. 1943. Top: Flattop's death, 1944. Like Poe and other Gothic entertainers, Chester Gould was obsessed with the idea of suffocation, the threat of being buried alive, whether in a deep well covered by a rock (Tracy himself); an ice-encrusted snowdrift (Krome); an underground cave (The Mole); or the muck in a garbage scow being towed out to sea (B-B Eyes), to cite some cases from the early forties. © 1944 Chicago Tribune–New York News Syndicate, Inc.

Detail, Papageorge's *New York City*.

shock of a Buna Beach. As recently as 1959, however, in *The Second World War* (Vol. II), Time-Life air-brushed the maggots off one soldier's back, an effacement very much in the American grain, like saying "passed away" instead of "died" or "dead." The sanitized image did not convince every reader that these resting fellows could pass for *Homo ludens,* to use the proper taxonomic tag—man playing, as the three boys regularly did in 1942, at the edge of Long Island Sound, waiting there after the invasion for someone to break the spell of play by calling, "Everybody up!"

The familiar still from *Yankee Doodle Dandy* breathes with life even now. The cardboard torch borne by the Statue of Liberty and the patent falseness of Uncle Sam's beard embody the spirit of play, a good thing to have in reserve, particularly if *Over There* comes here, where you are standing or sitting. The present writer, home from the hospital after a prolonged stay, unable to concentrate on written language, looked at picture books, television, and a large collection of old magazines hauled up from the basement by the children. Laurel and Hardy re-runs were the highlight of every afternoon. The boys are on the screen now, in old-fashioned black and white, playing beleaguered Foreign Legionnaires in North Africa. They've dropped their rifles and are doing a dreamy, slow-tempoed, soft-shoe routine.

Popular culture mobilized for World War II as rapidly as any industry, and observed its own laws. An adolescent radio hero such as Jack Armstrong was allowed to fight Nazi-controlled agents in the mountains of Chile while his comic book and movie coevals, the boy Commandos and Dead End Kids, were dispatched to more conventional war fronts. The war was covered best by *Life* magazine and Hollywood, "cover" and "front" here meaning propagandistic deception and false advertising. *Life*'s entire issue of July 7, 1941, was devoted to National Defense. Its main section, "The Arming of America," opened with this photograph (right). "Opening of a new defense plant [in Philadelphia] is today a patriotic occasion," reads the original caption. *Life*'s effort was perfectly coordinated. The film *Sergeant York,* a call to arms starring Gary Cooper, had just opened in New York, as had *Caught in the Draft,* with Bob Hope as an ex-movie star who suffers the comic indignities of basic training. His lowest point finds him in a mud hole, covered from head to foot with muck, but he rises to win the heart of the colonel's daughter, Dorothy Lamour, who is featured in *Life*'s Defense issue as the Army's "No. 1 Pin-up Girl." Four pages document the high-schoolish beach party given her by a youthful Coast Artillery unit in Hawaii. For "classier" fun, *Life* touts the luxurious Officer's Club at Fort Leavenworth, with its stables, polo field, golf course, tennis courts, and dinner dances. The club's kennels and "pink-coated Colonel Good, Master of the Hunt," are depicted in the warmly glowing colors of an English genre scene, but the most fanciful color page in the issue concerns basic army meals. Several overhead shots offer the most delicious-looking all-in-one trays in the history of American cafeterias and advertising. If it looks this way in a photo, it must be so. "The daily ration," declares the text, "is a dietetic triumph." "With its bright spots of color," states the caption for the chicken dinner, "this meal is also an aesthetic masterpiece of Army kitchen." *Dietetic triumph? Aesthetic masterpiece!* These words should have been hilarious, even in 1941, but the unambiguous rhetorical strength of the images must have reduced the text to a transparent irrelevancy. Henry Billings's painting of the U.S.S. *North Carolina,* a fantasy of irresistible power, is unquestionably the issue's aesthetic masterpiece (overleaf, left; originally in color). Bereft of people and shorn of handrails, ropes, rigging, and chimney smoke, this *North Carolina* aspires to the condition and aesthetic of monumental fascist sculpture and architecture, Death as a ship (whereas Papageorge's picture of defensive, exemplary war machines represents the other side).

Hollywood went even further than *Life.* In *This Is the Army* (1943), an adaptation of Irving Berlin's musical (overleaf, right), Warner Bros. turned the American eagle into a great big strong Nazi-like bird, a mere subliminal presence in the sky of Billings's picture, unless one takes the fearsome cloud formation for a giant B-17 bomber or wild goose. Redolent of Leni Riefenstahl's *The Triumph of the Will* (Germany, 1934), the stylized Uncle Sam looks deaf, dumb, and blind. How much like your enemy do you have to be in order to win a war? Hollywood's three hun-

Photographer unknown, *Opening of a New Defense Plant,* 1941.

Henry Billings, U.S.S. *North Carolina,* 1941. Original painting in color. © 1941 Time, Inc.

dred and fifty or so war-related movies produced between 1941 and 1945 follow and fulfill a remarkably strict set of self-imposed standards and conventions. Whether on land, sea, or air, every triumphant and concluding movie battle invariably cuts to a parade ground, where the hero receives a medal and then stands in review of a battalion of marching men, their steps accented by martial music and the sounds made by a phalanx of American flags snapping in the wind, a sight that used to bring a youthful audience to its feet, whistling and cheering. How they yearned to be given the same chance as Etta, Wonder Woman's chubby young pal, or Bucky, Captain America's sidekick, the first twelve-year-old to enlist. They never noticed that the flags are grainy stock-footage, an aesthetic mismatch.

Production number, *This Is the Army,* 1943. Original film in Technicolor.

Veterans of a nineteen-forties childhood usually view old World War II movies on TV with a mixture of nostalgia and dismay, not unlike the feelings we experience on Parent's Night at the neighborhood grammar school, when we lower ourselves, slowly and cautiously, down, down into our son or daughter's little desk chair, shifting and wriggling our bulk as decorously as possible until it is in place, the desk top forcing us to hunch over, toward our cramped knees. How long before the circulation will stop? How could we ever have been this small, so close to the ground yet so intense, especially about winning a distant war?

If a typical film of the period is on the screen, *Guadalcanal Diary* (1943), say, then the answer is clear: war films were pitched at a child's level. When *Caught in the Draft* deposited Hope in a mud hole, its shrewd investment was signal: war was going to be a load of laughs, an open-ended summer camp for boys. Everyone agreed. From *Wake Island* (1942) through *The Sands of Iwo Jima* (1949), movie marines joke and scrap among themselves like rambunctious campers or puppies; in *Guadalcanal Diary,* the youngest marine (Richard Jaeckel) sneaks a pup into combat. The Guadalcanal campaign is staged as the archetypal camp excursion. No girls are allowed, not even as nurses or as wives caught in quick flashbacks. Betty Grable appears once, as an 8-by-10-inch glamour glossy thumbtacked to a palm; these are not ca-

tamites. "They're a great bunch of kids," says their colonel, just after Jaeckel and William Bendix have wrestled on the deck of the troop ship. Bendix was thirty-seven at the time, and most of the other marines don't look much younger. They go into combat fearlessly and encounter none of the natural hazards of record, no giant crocodiles, huge wasps, spiders, centipedes, or tree-leeches. The terrors of jungle war are played for laughs of a very loaded sort: "I felt his buck teeth," says Bendix, after he has wrestled in the dark with a jagged palm frond. Even at summer camp a fellow can get hurt, or worse, and *Guadalcanal Diary* is most circumspect about the Big Sting, the Big Bite—the great American secret that is forever in search of a euphemism or hard-boiled metaphor. The first major casualties occur an hour into the 93-minute film, when a Marine platoon responds to a phony offer of surrender and is ambushed on an isolated beach (a true incident). By shooting the most grisly part of the ambush and its aftermath from the point of view of a survivor who has swum out to sea, the movie camera presents an acceptable version of *Life*'s close-up of Buna Beach.

Death is a long shot, literally. Four of the five major characters survive the campaign, as does the dog. Because bloody sand and water tend to discourage everyone, the film minimizes the terrific carnage inflicted on the Japanese defenders. The fun of the hunt is emphasized instead. When an invisible sniper

Helen Levitt, *New York City,* ca. 1940.

in a tree pins down a squad, one of the marines yells up in a gobbledygook nonsense-tongue. The puzzled sniper peers out of the foliage and is picked off. "Scratch one squint-eye," says the marine, as the sniper falls, shrieking "AIIIIIGHHH!!" (as it would be transliterated in a comic strip balloon). By erecting special recruitment booths outside theaters that were showing this film, the Marines were able to enlist 12,000 new recruits.

Helen Levitt photographed these impressionable boys in 1940 or so, in New York City (above). Their improvised headgear suggests that they have recently seen *Beau Geste.* We have grown since all that, by at least a foot—which is to say that we are still living in a visual culture, but not necessarily making much more sense of it than we did before. What do we make of images, and what have they made us do, or dream, or think, or remember?

In the nineteen-thirties and early forties, before TV, movies and moviegoing were frequently attacked for being detrimental to the health and well-being of their audiences. This photograph (right), taken on the set of *Beau Geste* (1939), proves incontestably (if proof is needed) that three of the boys in Helen Levitt's photo imagine themselves to be Ray Milland, Gary Cooper, and Robert Preston; the other Levitt boy, without a hat, is doing his Napoleon for the camera. A 1939 student and theorist of popular culture might well have forecasted a life of violence and misadventure for these boys, of frustrated romantic impulse. Such a supposition is not a caricature of the thinking of social scientists of the time; the most comprehensive campaign against the movies, the Payne Fund studies of the nineteen-thirties, suggests that there would be no sex without the influence of films. As early as 1919, a physician asserted that movies produced neuroses and organic disturbances such as Saint Vitus's Dance—an irrefutable statement to anyone who has read Nathanael West's *The Day of the Locust* (1939). In West's novel, the concluding riot at the movie premiere is staged as a kind of collective fit, an epidemic loss of motor control. People are kicked and bitten and, as West's surrogate in the novel, Tod Hackett, has his leg broken and is pushed into the air, he imagines the completion of his vast painting, "The Burning of Los Angeles," the author's apocalyptic vision of an impending civil war initiated by the lower middle class. According to West, they came to California expecting miracles, and now feel "cheated and betrayed," principally by their two major sources of distraction and titillation, the newspapers and the movies.

It was a shock for a democratically educated boy of the nineteen-forties to read this book at college in 1954 and to discover that motion pictures were scorned by estimable novelists and critics, many of whom admired *The Day of the Locust* as prophecy. The panic caused in 1938 by Orson Welles's famous *War of the Worlds* radio broadcast was an isolated and aberrant occurrence, but to a writer like West it must have symbolized the haplessness of the mass audience, who seem to be pleading for mercy in Edward Weston's *Rubber Dummies at the M-G-M Studio* (overleaf, right), photographed in 1939, the year of West's benchmark anti-Hollywood novel. Weston's staged symbolism is in fact ambiguous, but the dummies are obviously victims, whether they stand for Hollywood extras, average moviegoers, or "The Cheated" (to use West's working title for *The Day of the Locust*). Russell Lee depicts a more relaxed cou-

Beau Geste, 1939.

ple in his picture *Tenant Purchase Clients at Home, Hidalgo, Texas, 1939* (overleaf, left), made for the Historical Section of the Farm Security Administration (FSA), whose small staff of photographers proselytized for New Deal programs while showing Americans what America looked like during the years 1935–43. The Texas couple is wonderfully at ease, and at ease with popular culture. The same holds for Russell Lee, whose truly well-balanced picture miraculously skirts a cliché: the RCA ad, with the family gathered happily around the console radio, or the stock news shot of folks listening to one of

Russell Lee, *Tenant Purchase Clients at Home, Hidalgo, Texas, 1939.*

FDR's reassuring Fireside Chats. Lee exemplifies the democratic and populist spirit of the documentary tradition while Weston embodies the "elitist" point of view at its polar extreme, the fine arts tradition. Weston's debt here to the dolls and lifesize mannequins in well-publicized surrealist paintings and assemblages of the nineteen-thirties is blatant enough to suggest that a rich diet of art can be as

Edward Weston, *Rubber Dummies at the M-G-M Studio, Culver City, California, 1939.*

unhealthy as pop, to pun broadly in the style of James Joyce, who remains the archetypal, confounding high modernist in all the arts because his two great Irish stews blend the high and low so freely. "Stand up, mickos! Make strake for minnas!" he writes early in *Finnegans Wake* (1939), evoking a famous couple. Photographs should be looked at in this open, receptive, Joycean spirit.

The anti-Hollywood tone of the nineteen-thirties persists in works such as Bill Dane's *Hollywood 1974* (overleaf, left) and Les Krims's *The Static Electric Effect of Minnie Mouse on Mickey Mouse Balloons* (right), a vision from 1968, the year that Richard Schickel published *The Disney Version,* his negative assessment of their animated reality. Although Dane's inside view of a sculpture orgy is plainly funny (note the steamed-up mirror), the sculpture itself is "meretricious" and "tawdry," to invoke one dictionary's primary synonyms for "Hollywood," a pejorative title as clear as a verbal gloss in Hogarth (*Gin Lane,* for instance). Cupid and Psyche (second from left) have been cropped at the head and Rodin's *The Kiss* (left) has been gilded and compromised, the putative fate of art and artist alike in Hollywood. The photo was taken at Universal Studios. Most anti-Hollywood novels are dreary because the self-justifying screenwriter-novelists only try to demolish sitting targets, plaster-cast copies of venal producers and vain movie stars (for a welcome light touch, see Buster Keaton, ca. 1928, overleaf, right). Nathanael West has a genuine point of view, however, and his concern with seemingly ordinary people in *The Day of the Locust* has long made it exemplary to critics and readers who rarely question West's total animus toward every locust, Tod Hackett excepted. Krims is "Westian" to the extent that his latter-day Dadaism can make the viewer see that most everything is "Mickey Mouse" (i.e., corny, easy, simple-minded). Mass-produced religious artifacts are clearly "Mickey Mouse." So are pin-up poses, sexual coyness (Mickey and Minnie have been engaged for more than fifty years), programmed cuteness (Annette Funicello and the Mouseketeers on TV), studio portraits, and art photographs such as Edward Weston's. The awkward plank on the floor makes fun of the idea of Weston's elegantly composed lumber and carefully balanced trash can lid. Each Mickey Mouse balloon can be said to represent a jejune or pointless gesture, another pocket of hot air. Mickey Mouse may also be "Mickey Mouse" to Krims, though this judgment covers too many possibilities to mean very much.

During the nineteen-thirties and early forties, Disney was a critical as well as commercial success. H. G. Wells used to brag that he had introduced Charlie Chaplin to Disney, the creator of the other most famous face in the world, Mickey Mouse—a darling to intellectuals until his cartooned stick-figure was fleshed-out and idealized. The subsequent decline of Disney's reputation did not register on young children. Their most tender feelings continued to be formulated and developed by the surrogate children given to them by Disney in the guise of toys: Dumbo, poor motherless thing, who was hugged so hard that his stuffing frequently popped; Mickey Mouse, who was fed yellow-crayoned cardboard cheese and then covered for the night with his own blanket, a clean old dish rag; and Mickey's dog, Pluto, who was dragged everywhere by his pull-string and left underfoot, near the console radio, just beyond the view of Russell Lee's camera. If this is "Mickey Mouse," then nothing means anything—a fashionable stand in the nineteen-sixties.

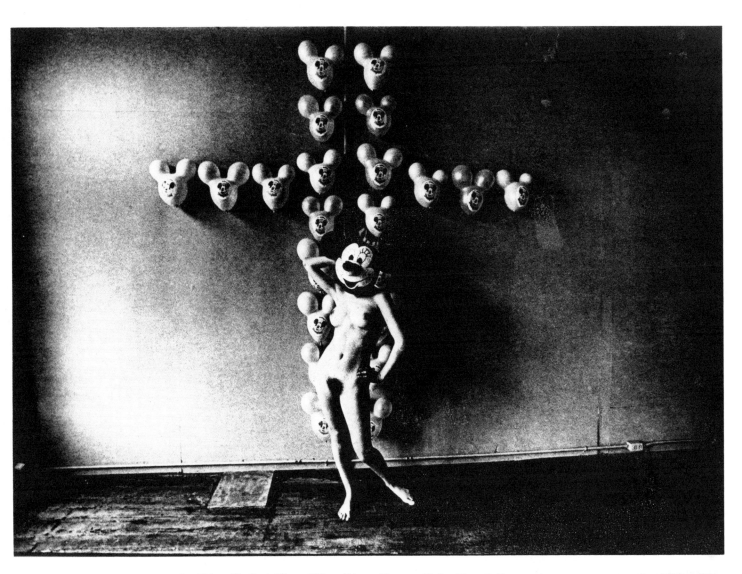

Les Krims, *The Static Electric Effect of Minnie Mouse on Mickey Mouse Balloons,* 1968.

Bill Dane, *Hollywood 1974.*

Witness the pervasive nihilism of the so-called Black Humorists of the period (Joseph Heller, Terry Southern, Kurt Vonnegut), and of West, their precursor, whose masterpiece, *Miss Lonelyhearts* (1933), floats and punctures a good many Mickey Mouse balloons of its own, Christianity foremost. If Krims's Playmouse of the Year seems too slim to warrant or support these remarks, they may be used instead to inflate yet another very small balloon. One must risk solemnity, however, because contemporary writers on photography are usually loath to compare its form or content with anything except other photographs. Such narrowness is "Strictly from Hunger," to interpolate the title of S. J. Perelman's classic 1942 send-up of Hollywood (an unhealthy place) and anti-Hollywood fiction (an overwrought genre).

Photographer unknown, Buster Keaton, ca. 1928.

Certain photographs should command as much attention as stories or novels, especially when the pictures amplify as well as complement the texts in question. *The Day of the Locust* must be amplified because it is widely accepted as a definitive work of social science, the last word on Hollywood. As a novel, however, it is too abstract and didactically charged. Its ordinary people are not really people, they are idiotic grotesques, splendidly etched. The old vaudevillian Harry Greener is a case in point. If he has a self, it's hidden by manic role-playing. "Harry, like many actors, had very little back or top to his head," writes West. "It was almost all face, like a mask," and its deep furrows "wouldn't permit degrees of feeling, only the furthest degree," an apt description of West's performance in *The Day of the Locust.* Harry's daughter Faye, an ambitious, platinum-tressed extra, is the eye of the storm in *Locust,* and her unearthly presence is replicated by this starlet, photographed at a 1956 premiere by Robert Frank for his epochal collection, *The Americans* (1959). Many of Frank's uncollected Hollywood images from this period are in the spirit of West, whose reputation was being revivified at about this time. In one picture, a winding staircase leading nowhere stands abandoned on a back movie lot. Another unsparing photograph depicts Mary Pickford the aging ex-star as an addled matron, two steps away from Frank's image of an old woman in Edwardian dress who is carrying a portrait of Rudolph Valentino (d. 1926) as she walks along on her annual pilgrimage to his grave. (See *Esquire,* March 1959, for this forgotten portfolio of pictures.)

"Faye Greener" (right) is equally Westian, but the camera is aimed at the middle ground ignored by West. "At the sight of their heroes and heroines, the crowd [at a premiere] would turn demoniac . . . then nothing but machine guns would stop it," writes West, near the end of the novel. Frank's bystanders still belong to humankind, and, read counter-clockwise, the responses of the three women in the crowd form a logical progression, moving from an uncomplicated smile on the right to a more inward and tentative smile beneath the "Squire's" sign and then to the pensive, apprehensive expression of the woman on the left, who is as solitary as one of Edward Hopper's movie ushers, even though photographs no longer have to look like paintings to be considered any good. Now they should resemble books. The woman's hand gesture is particularly arresting. The fourth woman, the starlet, completes the progression as inevitably as a concluding paragraph or chapter. Her dead Pan expression (West's pun, in *Miss Lonelyhearts*) represents his "furthest degree," a terminal stage of fantasy and frustration rendered demoniac here by the camera's diaphragm, which was opened to a wide aperture in order to focus on the crowd rather than on her; optically speaking, she is walking into trouble. She has good reason to be as doleful as Buster's mock-Venus: the bystanders are looking elsewhere, or through her, and if she were to glimpse herself in a mirror, this is how she would appear, given the

Robert Frank, *Movie Premiere, Hollywood,* 1956.

state of her eyes. Medical science tells us that she is suffering from cataracts, but since artists and writers of the grotesque use affliction as symbol and metaphor, the starlet can be said to represent the terrible essence of The Cheated at the end, when they surge and stumble through the streets blindly, like zombies. Hollywood has met photography in the foreground of Frank's picture. Film and photography meet here, too; the dynamism of frozen gesture and tension suggests that Frank, like Helen Levitt, would logically next turn to the making of non-theatrical motion pictures (her prize-winning documentaries *In the Street* [1945] and *The Quiet One* [1948] are considerably larger achievements than Frank's *Pull My Daisy* [1960]). If there are enough still pictures extant to constitute an anti-Hollywood genre in photography, from Weston to Dane, 1939 to 1974, then Frank's *Movie Premiere* has to be its masterpiece.

Photography is commonplace, yet individual photographs usually retain their little secrets because viewers do not look at them carefully enough. There are several reasons for this, the foremost having to do with a torpor created by visual pollution. Snapshots, news photos, TV broadcasts, ads of all sorts—we are surrounded and deluged by millions of images. Every event must be covered or uncovered, from the cradle to the Mardi Gras to the grave (right: John Gutmann, *The Game,* New Orleans, 1937; overleaf, right: the birth of Frank Sinatra, Jr., in Margaret Hague Hospital, Jersey City, New Jersey, a family scene photographed by Len Detrick for the New York *Daily News,* January 12, 1944). Intimacies beyond the ken of the picture press are depicted on TV "docu-dramas," those deceptively authentic and insidious improvements on the fictionalized film biographies of yore (overleaf, left: William Bendix as the title character in *The Babe Ruth Story* [1948], visiting Lou Gehrig on his death bed). We are spared almost nothing, yet learn little from what we see because a typical picture—a news image—is rarely art or news. The level of information in such pictures is very low; without a caption or voice-over, most of them would be ambiguous or meaningless. An immersion in such a visual culture does not develop good readers, of books or photographs.

Unfortunately, the scholars and critics of photography are more interested in history and theory than in the basic problems of literacy and interpretation. Educated viewers need more help than ever. In the nineteen-twenties and thirties, an elite audience could view in a handful of galleries such photographers as Steichen, Steiglitz, Strand, Man Ray, and Weston, and agree that their work should be accepted and understood on the same terms as modern art, whether that be Post-Impressionism, Cubism, Dada, or Surrealism. Everything else in the visual field belonged to mass culture, which demanded no close attention. Although the gap has narrowed between the art photograph and the vernacular and documentary genres, many critics and reviewers still insist upon traditional distinctions: the quotidian photo as history or sociology rather than psychology, as fact rather than symbol. Russell Lee's radio (p. 24) must only carry Depression programs; the "Plus" on his Chicago ticket booth (p. 2) is nothing more than a visual fragment. One such critic regards Robert Frank's starlet as "a metaphor of vulgarity." The starlet may well be vulgar, but not here. She's too wraithlike to qualify—Vulgarity ought to have eyes, if not a great big Pop Art smile—and the focus is literally on the people behind her. The sociologizing critic ignores them, and the pensive woman on the left, who might not be happy to know that her unguarded expression has been caught and preserved forever. Evidently quotidian photographers must work like burglars and purse-snatchers and spies to earn our respect as artists or reporters.

Street practitioners such as Helen Levitt and Ben Shahn often used a right-angle viewfinder, which gave their subjects the impression that the photographers were aiming their cameras elsewhere. Robert Frank went unnoticed by the crowd at the premiere be-

John Gutmann, *The Game (New Orleans)*, 1937.

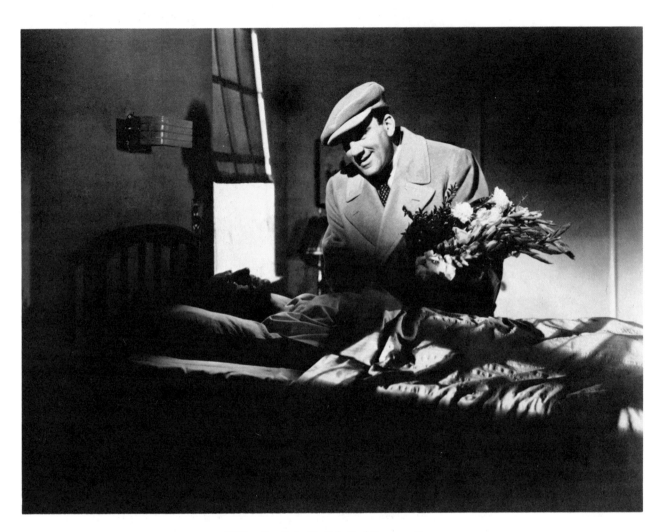

William Bendix in *The Babe Ruth Story,* 1948.

cause he seemed to be shooting the starlet, not them. The expression on the bystander's face points to Frank's skill and the deepest fears of everyone: they'll read my mind if I'm not careful. Filed under the rubric of "social studies," Frank's picture demonstrates that the reach of a photograph should not be determined or circumscribed by its ostensible subject and genre. Vulgarity is skin-deep for the nonce.

By titling this photo *The Game,* John Gutmann refused to be solemn about social self-consciousness

Len Detrick, *The Birth of Frank Sinatra, Jr.,* 1944.

and the idea of social display as subterfuge and artifice. Would a battery of news photographers be able to discover if the effete central figure is male or female? The player on the right is smiling confidently because she knows that the camera cannot strike through the mask of appearance here. Mask is the key word. *"Strike through the mask!"* the instructor tells his students in Communications 101, "Street and Documentary Photography," borrowing his injunction from Melville's Ahab.

Simon Nathan, *Weegee Covering the Opera,* 1945.

If one looks twice at this news photo by the free-lance photojournalist Simon Nathan (above), it should be clear that it documents a psychological rather than a social fact about the human race: its instinct for self-protective privacy. Unambiguous and direct, Nathan's image can stand on its own, without a title or caption, though it helps if one is familiar with the work of Weegee (b. Arthur Fellig), who is shown here (center) as he covers an opening night at the Metropolitan Opera House in 1945, the year of his best-selling picture-book, *Naked City.* The title is a cliché now, but it summarizes the rending effect of Weegee's flashgun and highly expressive pictures, from his compassionate shots of fire victims to his witty and cruel eviscerations of fatuous operagoers. By his own estimate, Weegee covered five thousand murders; they were the free-lancer's principal stock-in-trade, particularly during the era of Murder, Inc. Weegee sought three basic images at the scene of a crime: the bloody victim, lying in the street (see p.

14); the bystanders, variously amused, grieved, bored, and horrified; and the perpetrator or prime suspect, a bruised fellow being led away by the police. Sometimes, with luck, Weegee would capture two of these images in one picture, but never all three. Simon Nathan has produced a perfect Weegee here: victim, bystanders, and the perpetrator, Weegee himself, fingered by the bloodless victim, who is still on his feet but aghast at the prospect of seeing his picture in the paper. While other young men his age are in the army or navy, fighting a war, he's at the opera, sporting white gloves, an outré fur coat, and an expensive razor-trimmed head of hair. Who's gonna get him first? Weegee, of course. The taut expression on the chauffeur's face defines the seriousness of the confrontation between his boss and Weegee, whose expression says, "Who, *me?* I meant no harm. I'm innocent!" The smile of the photographer on the left clearly belongs to a guilty figure, Weegee's Doppelgänger. His smile would be good-natured in the context of Mrs. Sinatra's room, but here it is malignant, manifesting as it does the most aggressive bad motives of photography, the pitiless spirit of the paparazzi. Only a newborn baby (Mrs. Sinatra's) could be ready and braced for an explosion of flashbulbs above his bed.

Invasion of privacy is a graphic enough phrase, connoting warfare and grievous personal injury. Anyone who has watched an amateur street photographer at work on a busy thoroughfare knows that people rarely smile for the candid camera; children are an exception, as in Helen Levitt's *Beau Geste*

document. If the photographer makes himself conspicuous by holding his ground as he snaps his exposures, a majority of the passersby will drop their gaze, turn away, duck, or hold up a hand, as though everyone in town was a Weegee subject, wanted by the F.B.I., or deathly afraid of cameras. In *King Kong,* a remake with a point of view (1976), the beast breaks through his cage and runs amok in New York when he thinks that the flashbulbs of the photographers are hurting his beloved blonde starlet (Jessica Lange). The strobes blaze and flash against the darkness like flame-throwers and machine guns, a compressed vision of Susan Sontag's well-known indictment of photography and its aggressiveness, which is old news in one way: anthropologists have long noted the atavistic fears of so-called primitive peoples who believe that a photograph steals one's soul. Does the outraged operagoer know that this is the celebrated Weegee, whose most famous picture, *The Critic* (1943), depicts two silly-looking operagoing dowagers receiving a Bronx cheer from an Apple Annie bag-lady? Does the fellow have something to be embarrassed about, such as a huge and ugly nose? Is he wearing a tastefully applied mask of white powder or makeup? Is this why he's not in the army? Will his chauffeur come to his rescue in a second or two? What is he saying to Weegee? Could the hatless boy be asking, in Helen Levitt's photograph, "Why you wanna take our pitcher, lady?" The interrogative mode is well-suited to photography. These rhetorical questions are irrelevant, finally, for Simon Nathan has captured an open-ended drama.

When a photograph is notably deficient in information or drama, the viewer can say that the image is as inscrutable and mysterious as masked reality, and leave it there, or dismiss it altogether as trivial, banal, and boring. This has often been said of the most unprepossessing documentary or street photographs of Lee Friedlander, who took this picture (right) in Louisiana in 1968. It is not an arresting or immediately accessible photograph. When we look at Simon Nathan's photo of Weegee et al. our eyes read naturally from left to right and then back again, quickly discerning the basic tensions in the picture; the action, after all, is confined to the foreground. To read from left to right in Friedlander's photo is to move from nothing to not very much and then—well, certainly not back again. Where to now? What catches our attention and why? The unfamiliar SPUR sign? Is it a regional brand of gasoline? Is this the kind of question an adult should ask, or is it the ontological equivalent of beer can collecting? The sign is a commercial eyesore, of an international sort, but that subject is too familiar to merit further comment, if it is indeed the subject here. Something must redeem or at least recommend this scene. Why is it in a book, or on display in a gallery or museum? The shadow of the majorette! It looks like one of Matisse's graceful and monumental cut-outs, done about 1952, but, alas, the analogy doesn't lead anywhere. What about the majorette? Is she leading a parade? It looks more like she's a parade of one, a figure of fun strutting her stuff in some fantasy of "sexiness" as self-enclosed as the circumscribing triangle formed by the edge of the telephone pole and the diagonal shadow of the other pole. Caught this way, with the white-helmeted soldiers and most of the children looking down the street, away from her, the majorette is almost as alone as Robert Frank's movie starlet (p. 31). *Soldiers?* In riot helmets, too. What's happening down the street? Could it be a Civil Rights demonstration? "Nothing," the left-hand part of the scene, could turn out to be something: the setting for the convergence of two parades, or opposing forces, Left and Right.

Friedlander has willfully rejected all public events here, asserting their evanescence by using his camera to disrupt the flow of the alleged parade, as though he were one of those (nihilistic?) modern novelists who refuses to offer a linear narrative, a panoramic view of society, an omniscient cause-and-effect explanation of events and behavior. The American flag at the center of the scene is inert and barely visible, as if to reinforce the picture's personal perspective, its remove from any *Life*-based allegiance to the official culture (p. 17). The action here is in the foreground, after all; in fact, it is foregrounded. By self-consciously (that is, self-reflexively) photographing his own shadow on the telephone pole this way, the photographer has once again called attention to and questioned his procedures and (solipsistic?) mission, his own fantasies of ideal form (see his 1970 book of photographs, *Self Portraits,* where the hulking shadow of the photographer either fills the frame to no purpose—the village idiot at play—or stalks its prey like Frankenstein and the Phantom of the Op-

Lee Friedlander, *Lafayette, Louisiana,* 1968.

era, the first-nighter's perception of Weegee in Nathan's picture). The shadow here belongs at once to Peeping Tom, who was struck blind for glancing at Lady Godiva when she rode by, and to Friedlander, who has used a mere telephone pole to anchor a surprisingly neat network of diagonal and vertical lines. There are no less than twelve poles before us. Conjure a breeze, look at those flags! What a grand day! To impose a bit of hopeful fancy or a rudimentary sense of design on such a jerry-built and stultifying scene is of course not the same as making com-

plete sense of it, an ambition more within the purview of the nineteenth-century novelist (past and present) than the contemporary documentary photographer, if "documentary" is the right word for this kind of street picture. A definition or distinction: street photography is to documentary photography what jazz improvisation is to the recognizable, clearly stated melody. If this is too breezy, then: Helen Levitt's *Beau Geste* is a documentary photo insofar as it demonstrates the impact of movies—and a "street photograph" by virtue of its choreography of gesture.

What is a documentary photograph and where does the self figure in a photo? These are not simple questions, but they can be answered simply, to provide a point of departure. The dictionary says that documentary means "objective," "factual," "representational." In photography, the Farm Security Administration offers the best example of a successful documentary enterprise. (Its most celebrated photographer, Walker Evans, always preferred the term "documentary style," by which he meant a naturalistic rather than arty approach to the photographic subject.) Under the leadership of Roy E. Stryker, the FSA staff sought to realize in holistic series of images the primary definition of documentary: "contained or certified in writing." An FSA photographer went into the field armed with one of Stryker's "shooting scripts." These offered detailed suggestions of things to photograph, from close-ups of poor people's clothes and shoes to the various ways different social classes spend their evenings. Russell Lee's photo of the Texas couple is a documentary masterpiece and a great picture because it is a timeless symbol as well as a realist's descriptive statement (p. 24). *Life*'s picture of the flag-wavers is certainly a symbol, thanks in part to its caption (p. 17), but it will not pass muster as a documentary photograph. By trying to include as many of the workers as possible, the photographer has failed to describe the range of social classes represented here, their faces and clothing, their need of employment as opposed to their "patriotism." Many are not even smiling, which suggests that the "celebration" has been produced by the plant's publicity director,

who may have distributed the free flags and instructed everyone to wave at the cameras. The photo would be a more convincing image if, instead of M. WILSON ENGINEERS, the sign said DEFEND AMERICA.

Verbal clues can be misleading, however, as in this FSA photo (right) by Ben Shahn, captioned *Street Scene, Washington Court House, Ohio, 1938.* If the picture had been titled "Capital Loan," the viewer would be certain that it documents the plight of this farmer, who is in debt to the bank. Time is running out for him (clock symbolism by John Steinbeck). His posture, however, does not support this surmise. The modest truth about the picture is in fact defined by the framed placard on the right, containing four captioned news photos of the second Joe Louis–Max Schmeling fight. A national news service provided eight pictures each week to subscribers until around 1956. The farmer is studying the other set of news photos. Shahn's picture documents the dissemination of information, which includes the correct time of day. Although the reflections in the window may be diverting, Shahn is not interested in spatial ambiguities; he shot this on the run, as is made clear by the reflection of the photographer (left), aiming his right-angle viewfinder. Shahn should not be confused here with Lee Friedlander or any other self-conscious artist, film director, or writer who deliberately inserts himself in his work. This happens in no other Shahn photo and, conceptually speaking, there was no place for the self in Roy Stryker's objective sphere. For self-projection, Shahn had his paintings. In *Self-Portrait among Churchgoers,* 1939, a street

Ben Shahn, *Street Scene, Washington Court House, Ohio, 1938.*

scene based on several photos, Shahn painted himself in action as a photographer, snapping the dour churchgoers. The message written on the sermon bulletin board in the painting didactically underscores the artist's intention and total control of his medium. Self-expression in photography is problematic, but the problem belongs to the photographer, not the viewer. This viewer stirred the flags reflexively in Friedlander's slice of Louisiana because that's the way a parade should look, as we know from real life and old movies and photos, commingled in memory as personal pictures.

We are always open to photographs and should feel more at home there than in any other form, or form of art, and why not? Everyone has been in a photograph. When we scrutinize an impersonal photo we sometimes find more of ourselves there than when we look in a mirror, unless the mirror catches us by surprise, the way a photographer might, his flashgun forcing us to drop our presumptuous and protective pronouns. That could be me in Shahn's picture, an easily diverted person, twentieth-century man getting a truncated version of the news, and wearing overalls for the first time.

A photograph may be problematic simply because its resonant action can be overlooked so easily by viewers who settle too quickly for charm instead of insight. Observe *Children at the Blackboard, Lake Dick Project, Arkansas, April 1939*, photographed for the FSA by Russell Lee (right). The children are barefooted and hence poor, but they are clean and neatly dressed, reflecting their parents' pride and respect for the idea of school and a formal education. Their hair is freshly cut, combed, and brushed, clear signs of discipline and self-respect. The picture is typical of the work of Russell Lee, a notably selfless and unaggressive photographer who seems to have moved through rooms as though he were a trusted member of the family (p. 24) or an invisible man, the perfect guest. His ostensible intention in this shot, one of a series, was to show the new Lake Dick Project being put to good use, right down to the draft-free baseboard and government-bought chalk. The little girl on the far right wields her chalk with a determination made compelling by the fact that she has the poorest dress and is the only one with a suntan, the result, probably, of her having had to help with the March plowing and April planting. Someone has said that man has to learn two things— to communicate and to die; the girl on the right is doing very well already, at least with the former. The same cannot be said of everyone here. It must be their first day with the first letter, for the boy on the left has re-created the history of the *A*, from its origins on a cave wall to its appearance in first grade. When he steps back from the board and compares his with the other *A*'s, will he see that all men are not created equal? If lettering is destiny, is the future projected on the board before them? Are patterns of personality being determined right here, for Lee's camera? Or are they already set, apparent, and in motion? The little girl who is bending down would be the star of her class if they had been asked to draw a wishbone or tweezers. It's no joke to her, however. Note how she gave up momentarily and wrote a small *a,* then tried the capital letter again, and then knocked over a piece of chalk. She suffers from more than poor motor control. The fact that she is writing with her right hand but reaching with her left doubtless points to the kind of deep left/right confusion that, unresolved by one of the two hemispheres of the brain, often results in the learning disability now known as dyslexia. She may have dropped the chalk on purpose—*anything* to delay the process at the board and reduce the born loser's sense of shame. Is the girl on her right encouraging her or teasing her? She is the fastest letterer by far, the best dressed, the tallest, and probably the fastest runner, too, and here I'm drawing on the biological grammar-school fact that girls are often bigger and stronger than boys.

She's teasing her, I think. "Moron!" whispered the tall boy seated to my right as I finished reading aloud from our second-grade primer. I had delivered my two sentences fairly well until the last word, "sing," which I declaimed as "snig"—a sign of my own dyslexia. I suffered from such reversals for the first four grades. During our old-fashioned reading drills,

Russell Lee, *Children at the Blackboard, Lake Dick Project, Arkansas, April 1939.*

which were conducted seat by successive seat, two times a day, I would look ahead in the text, figure out which two sentences would be mine, study and rehearse them, and, through guesswork, sometimes circumvent these reversals. But if a stellar speed-reader seated one or two desks ahead of me was awarded an encore, and performed three more sentences rapidly, I felt sick because I wouldn't have time to —my turn! "Uh . . . Where are we?" I'd say, pretending to lose my place, my heart pounding like hoofbeats in a movie or radio program, two places where almost nothing could get by me. My eyes are riveted on the sentence, trying to divine the truth about the minefield before me.

There is nothing problematic about this picture, taken by Ben Shahn in 1935 for the FSA (right). Save for the sign in English, these fellows could be almost anywhere; the locus happens to be the town of Omar on Scott's Run, West Virginia, which is coal mining country. The action, such as it is, is universal; every reader-viewer is wearing overalls now. As boys, we also studied the movie stills outside our theater, the Playhouse—two or three times a week, but especially on Tuesdays, when the midweek show arrived. Unless it was vacation time, we could never see these films, and their stills glowed with the aura of forbidden knowledge. We passed the Playhouse at least twice a day for six years on our way to and from the neighborhood grammar school (1941–46). On warm mornings the side exit doors were kept open while they cleaned the theater, and we often wished aloud that some weekend night we might find one of these doors open. The school was only one block from the Playhouse, a fitting conjunction, for movies and an occasional copy of *Life* or *Look* filled in some of the largest gaps in our bland and secular middle-class curriculum and culture—the subject of death, for one. Where country boys and coal miners' sons could encounter and ponder death in the woods or at the end of the company street, suburban children mainly looked to the screen, where the demise of Gary Cooper, say, in *Pride of the Yankees,* was more real than the discreet passing of one's grandmother over there, in some distant nursing home. Although Cooper swung the bat too stiffly as the *healthy* Gehrig and ran the bases in a sissyish, knock-kneed fashion, he

did enact Gehrig's sudden symptoms and decline convincingly enough to mist many eyes at the Playhouse, especially during a domestic scene in which Lou cannot finish tying his own bow tie, and his young wife (Teresa Wright) has to do it for him, smiling as though nothing were the matter. But Babe Ruth almost stole the show, playing himself, the Bambino, the élan vital, perpetual motion incarnate, whether he was hugging Cooper in a re-creation of a famous news photo of Gehrig's farewell ceremony at Yankee Stadium; wolfing down a dozen hot dogs; ripping off the jackets and shirts of teammates at a victory celebration; roaring, and laughing, and smashing a new straw boater over its owner's head.

Yet *Pride of the Yankees* was not altogether gripping or satisfying. Failing to understand that they were watching the life of a stoical, secular saint—an excellent example for the troops overseas—many of the boys in the Playhouse were simply bored by the slow-paced, asexual courtship scenes. Faked coughs and scattered catcalls from the audience marred at least one genuinely sweet scene. The chief matron, "Mrs. Pruneface," a battle-axe in nurse's white, tried to silence the malcontents, most of them spotted within the roped-off confines of the under-twelve kiddy section (the far sides of the two main aisles and the first fifteen rows of the auditorium). A re-release of *Little Caesar* engaged and held everyone's attention a few weeks later. It was the closing feature on a notably clamorous four-hour Saturday matinee that included a Western, dandy explosions in the weekly newsreel, several cartoons, the *Batman* serial, a boring travel-

Ben Shahn, *Omar on Scott's Run, West Virginia, 1935.*

ogue (hail of spitballs and wadded candy wrappers), and then, finally, the famous gangster film. Its depiction of the rise and fall of Edward G. Robinson awed us completely, more so, perhaps, than its original audience of 1930 because we had seen Robinson assert and reconfirm his unwavering toughness in so many subsequent roles. "Mother of Mercy, is this the end of Rico?" he asks as he dies in the alley, his use of the third person at once rendering the death of the tender ego and a conceptual leap from self to society, to *us,* seated there in the dark, perceiving, wondering, stunned. *"The show is over!"* The lights are on. Mrs. Pruneface is yelling at us to move. I am staring at the screen, a blank space now. The ushers are throwing open the side doors to air the place for the evening show. I don't want to leave this room.

SIGNS OF LIFE

Russell Lee, *Saturday Afternoon Street Scene, Welch, West Virginia, Aug. 24, 1946.*

Serious contemporary photographers of quotidian subjects want their pictures to stand alone, and mean whatever you think they mean. There was a time, however, roughly 1935–55, when documentary photographers sought to include signs in their pictures, either as bits of information or glosses on the content. The "content" and "meaning" inherent in a given scene can be shifted easily enough. If Dorothea Lange had come upon this scene, she would have moved in quickly, on the left, to photograph the husky black man as he passed beneath TROUBLE. Louis Faurer would have moved closer, allowed the men to pass, and then photographed a tense space built around the film title at the top and the blank faces of the three (troubled? glum?) teenagers on the left, cropped at the neck. Forgoing the sign, Robert Frank would have moved close enough to snap the teenagers against the display of shoes behind them, as if to say, "New things will not save them" (documentary photography invariably seems to reach for words). Walker Evans, the great American master of the documentary style, would have moved closer again to take a head and chest shot of the teenagers, to catch the exact nuances of their expressions; these signs and architecturally dull buildings would not have suited Evans's sensibility. Henri Cartier-Bresson, the begetter, with André Kertész, of the small camera, international-street style, would have hoped for something more definite by or under the "BORN FOR TROUBLE" sign—*Zut!* too bad those kids are not bums, or nuns—and then he'd have headed for the smoky hills above the town.

As it is here (left), photographed by the even-handed Russell Lee, the film title is one neutral component of *Saturday Afternoon Street Scene, Welch, West Virginia, Aug. 24, 1946*—almost a year after the official end of World War II. If *The Best Years of Our Lives* had been playing at the Pocahontas Theatre, Lee might well have skipped the scene altogether since the fulsome *Best* would have worked ironically against the averageness of the street and spoken authoritatively for Hollywood alone, whose attendance figures would reach an all-time high by the end of 1946. A

twenty-first century student of significant American ephemera can be assured that the whole range of signs in Lee's picture is typical and representative, right down to the girl's new saddle shoes, which, whether they came from the store on the left or Florsheim's up the street, document post-war optimism if not prosperity. The small traffic jam signals the end of gas rationing, and a newfound American mobility, while the theater sign represents the apogee of Hollywood in American life, and the idea of moviegoing as a community activity. The town of Welch, it should be said, had a 1940 population of 6,200. It's apt that the Temple cinema is housed in the sturdy Odd Fellows Temple Lodge, a fraternal organization similar to the Masons; this fact may not be apparent to everyone, even now. While the putative twenty-first century viewer should have no trouble with native names like Pocahontas and Firestone, the incomplete Odd Fellows sign may throw him off course or mislead him entirely, explaining in part why contemporary photographers now try to avoid having "literary" support systems within or around their images. Recent retrospective volumes devoted to the work of Walker Evans and Cartier-Bresson have banished all captions to the back of the book, lest art be mistaken for photojournalism or transient, topical documentary stuff.

What's in a sign on a movie theater? Royal and majestic names once prevailed, as befitted the opulence of Amerian movie palaces, especially those that were built in the nineteen-twenties. The lettering of the signs was usually plain enough, but everything else was exuberant, grand, and florid, from the tiled mosaic floors by the ticket booths (Lee's photo, p. 2) to the starry skies of the auditoriums. Almost every style of decoration and architecture was used in the movie palaces, ranging from the Persian, Hindu, and Egyptian to the Romanesque and Baroque (see the filigree on the ticket booth); sometimes they were all visible in one structure, an escapist spectacle as outrageous and fantastic as any film the management could ever present there—*The Thief of Bagdad* (1924), say, in which Douglas Fairbanks flew over the city on a magic carpet.

The awe that could be inspired by a theater alone is best expressed by a Helen Hokinson *New Yorker* cartoon from 1929. "Mama, does God live here?" asks a little boy on his first visit to New York City's Roxy Theatre (1927–60), which seated five thousand people—and people is the operative word. Chicago's vast Paradise Theatre served them well (1929–56), and serves us still, in memory, as part of a model environment. Its lower floor included several restaurants, a merry-go-round, and a kind of day-care center for the benefit of mothers who wished to deposit their children there before the show—a shrewd business idea that only in retrospect points to the idea of city-building as a humane activity. Unlike the Roxy, the Paradise was located in an area of the city that was both residential and commercial (Crawford Avenue near Washington Boulevard). An elevated train three blocks from the theater provided transportation, though most of the audience lived in the tree-lined neighborhood and walked to the show. The Paradise had no parking lot, and none of the local businesses, apartment buildings, or houses was more than three or four stories high, which made Crawford Avenue the same as 2nd Street (right), the main thoroughfare of Ashland, Wisconsin, photographed by Stephen Shore in 1973 (1970 population: 9,615, or 1,500 fewer than in 1940). The building on the right is the public library; the post office, Masonic Temple, Knights of Columbus, and courthouse are all within two or three blocks of the well-balanced Bay Theater, where moviegoing is part of the natural order of things. Named by an unimaginative or pantheistic owner after nearby Chequamegon Bay, the theater opened in 1938, offering Ashland an up-to-date alternative to its two old movie houses, the rundown Majestic, home of B-Westerns, and the very staid Royal, once a "legit" theater. The Bay's marquee is Art Deco, the thirties style most closely associated with the putative glamour of large cities and transatlantic travel.

How did people react to the Bay when it opened? "With wonder and delight," says John Szarkowski, who grew up in Ashland and was happy to reminisce about its movie houses. "It reminded everyone of an ocean liner. Nobody had ever seen one, of course. Only pictures." If this picture had been in black and white, however, the Bay and perhaps Ashland too

Stephen Shore, *Bay Theater, 2nd Street, Ashland, Wisconsin, 1973*.

would appear to be a drab place now, possibly as burnt-out as all those dead light bulbs on the scalloped edge of the Art Deco waterfall. "And you'd miss that special northern Wisconsin light," says Szarkowski. We may well miss too much as it is, especially the information about 2nd Street, which Stephen Shore might have imparted had he chosen to shoot the scene from Russell Lee's instructive West Virginia vantage point. This assumes, of course, that the buildings are clearly marked by signs or style. But Shore is not a documentary photographer; he is interested in the scene as a formal spatial unit, warmed or made perfect by light. Perhaps if that special Wisconsin light could be reproduced here with utter fidelity, it would serve as a luminous manifestation of the word-bound ideals we are celebrating somewhat hesitantly as we try to keep sentimentality at bay, or defuse it with wordplay.

Ben Shahn, *Omar on Scott's Run, West Virginia, 1935.*

A typical FSA photograph of the thirties juxtaposes a poor person and a cheerful sign, billboard, or poster, proof enough that "we are two nations," as Dos Passos concluded in *U.S.A.* (1938). The photographers themselves are more distinctive than this, however. Although Dorothea Lange's sign-bearing images are inevitably mordant and ironic, pure social protest, those of her friends Russell Lee and Ben Shahn are often extraordinarily tender and sweet. The signs and sentiments in such photographs would be deemed too overt for words were they to turn up in a contemporary painting or story. Witness Shahn's 1935 photos of Omar, West Virginia (above), or of a country fair in central Ohio, 1938. A close-up of the Omar scene (p. 45) clearly indicates that it is a coal mining town (1940 population: 1,353); the haze may well be coal dust. Even the movie is about coal mining, hardly everyone's idea of "escapism." But the four boys in the photo are not put off by *Hard Rock Harrigan,* the latest version of Coals to Newcastle. The innocent and eager posture of the boys is shared by the crowds at the Ohio country fair. In one photograph, a group of bystanders gawks at the "Side Show," four ordinary-looking men and women displayed beneath a banner promising the audience STRANGE PEOPLE and SENSATIONS FROM ALL PARTS [of the world? The edge of the banner is hidden]. In another view of the scene, a woman is transfixed by a banner depicting the PERSONALITY FAT GIRL, admission 10¢, the same as a movie. If Norman Rockwell, Stevan Dohanos, or any of the other illustrators for *The Saturday Evening Post* had based some pictures on these scenes, the resulting images might be dismissed now as sentimental and condescending. Shahn could not have escaped such criticism had he made a painting of Russell Lee's married couple (p. 24). The woman is far too gross, and she would never have posed in a hair net and curlers, not even in Hidalgo, Texas (1940 population: 693). Her laceless shoes are bathetic, and the enormous (what else?) hole in the man's sock is surely one touch too many, an outrageous plea for sympathy. The smoothly contoured floor model Art Deco radio is too clearly the center of their lives, and did it have to be so grand, the fireside equivalent of Radio City Music Hall? And isn't the irony of the sampler on the wall a bit heavy-handed, with its bewigged denizens gathered around a harpsichord instead of a radio? The steadfast symmetry and balance of the remainder of the mise-en-scène is too programmatic, as is the highly allusive name of the Omar Theatre and the "literary" division of space in this picture. The boys are sheltered and relaxed, but the men are in the open, on dangerous ground, recalling Hemingway's "The Three Day Blow," from *In Our Time* (1925), which places the fathers outdoors, at the center of the storm, the boys indoors, knowing that their time will come. The reality of the mines quite literally lurks behind the theater in the picture. The staircase of the Omar and the line into the tunnel define dramatically opposed forces in their lives. Hard rock indeed! The sole decorative star above the entrance here could also be military insignia on an army outpost or aid station. "Come, fill the Cup," states *The Rubáiyát* of Omar Khayyám, whose carpe diem theme is painfully apposite. Although the Omar photos might be unacceptable if they were "socially conscious" paintings, the photographic truth cannot be gainsaid. Save for the top of the "marquee," there are no soft contours in the two pictures. Who, except possibly a Marxist, would call moviegoing in Omar a frivolous diversion? "Ah, make the most of what we yet may spend, / Before we too into the Dust descend." To quote these lines from *The Rubáiyát* is to belabor the point, the way Shahn sometimes did when he transformed one of his own quietly eloquent photos into a painting that proclaims its humanism in very loud colors or large letters.

The signs in certain FSA photographs of the Depression indicate that entertainment was no less important than religion to hard-pressed people. Preston Sturges reaches this conclusion in *Sullivan's Travels* (1941), his satire of a successful Hollywood director who aspires to make a socially relevant film, *Brother, Where Art Thou?* To gather material, Sullivan (Joel McCrea) goes on the bum, quite comfortably, but his charade gets out of hand and he ends up on a wretched chain gang in the deep South. One night he and the other prisoners, a bitter and listless crew, are brought to an old-time Negro country church, where the hymn-singing congregation and the convicts are shown a nameless Disney animated cartoon featuring Pluto. The dog's comic battles with a sheet of sticky flypaper and a recalcitrant window shade elicit great laughter in the church as even the most demoralized convicts come to life (the sequence is from *Playful Pluto* [1934], the closest Disney gets to the Keaton-Chaplin level). Amazed, Sullivan sees the light: entertainment is quite enough. "It's all some people have in this cockeyed caravan," he says as the film ends, following his rescue. It is easy to understand why some viewers and critics have found this to be an unsatisfying rationalization or apologia, yet the picture files of the FSA reinforce Sturges's position (see Hank O'Neal's *A Vision Shared* [1976], pp. 40, 41, 154, 250–51). Sometimes the source of awe or wonder in these scenes is "incredible," to quote Ben Shahn. In October 1935, in the town square of impoverished Huntingdon, Tennessee (1940 population: 1,432), Shahn took a series of photos of a so-called medicine show. The salesman of patent medicine holds the attention of the stolid crowd, somehow. He is assisted by a melancholy and weary-looking old black man whose mouth is made over with the grotesque white lips of a minstrel performer. Another picture of the show offers a close-up of the third (and central?) member of the cast, a grimy and battered little black ventriloquist dummy dressed like a prisoner on a chain gang, shackles included—a potential Preston Sturges scenario for Edgar Bergen's Charlie McCarthy. A third photo of the crowd shows many of the men smiling, but there is no Pluto in sight for the black assistant and his wooden Doppelgänger, not in this town, anyway. A week or so later in Natchez, Mississippi, Shahn photographed another doleful black man, an aging one-legged shoe-shine boy seated next to a sign announcing "Harlem's Society/Presents 'Joe Louis Celebration'/O. Smith's Orch.," and this was two years before Louis became champion. His major victories were at once national news (see p. 40) and the occasion for jubilation in black neighborhoods, where crowds in the street would sometimes get a bit too enthusiastic to suit the sensibilities of white onlookers, especially in the South. By 1939, when Marion Post Wolcott photographed this theater (right) in Leland, Mississippi (1940 population: 3,700), Louis was the indisputable Rex (if not ℞) for colored people, proclaimed "King Joe" by Paul Robeson on a recording with Count Basie's Orchestra (1941). The Rex Theatre is separate but equal, to use the jargon of segregation; its ostensible feature films, two B-Westerns, are no

Marion Post Wolcott, *Rex Theatre for Colored People, Leland, Mississippi, 1939.*

worse than the fare at the Omar or the Big Boy Williams "Shoot-'em-up" at the Lyric Theatre (next page). But a look at the fine print here reveals three posters advertising a short devoted to Louis's bout with Bob Pastor, a white man, as were most of his opponents. Inasmuch as Louis knocked him out in the eleventh round, it's safe to say that on this day and evening, the Rex was separate and superior. Only brick walls could have muffled and contained the audience's joyous and risky subversive clamor. Did such fight films bring the saddest black men back to life? To know that, one needs another sign, at least.

Berenice Abbott, *Lyric Theatre, Third Avenue, New York City,* 1936.

To record social attitudes and historical facts not easily captured by any camera, documentary photographers of the thirties and forties often relied on scenes which boasted highly informative signs or posters. AIR [the word painted by hand in large, bold letters]/AIR/THIS IS YOUR/COUNTRY DONT/LET THE BIG/MEN TAKE IT/AWAY/FROM YOU, declares the sign on a tire pump photographed by Dorothea Lange in Kern County, California, 1938. "LORD'S PRAYER/ENGRAVED ON/YOUR PENNY/5¢," reads a sign in

Donaldsville, Louisiana, taken by Russell Lee in 1938, the same year he found this announcement borne by a cigar-store Indian outside a little shop in Pine Bluff, Arkansas: "DR. R. B. WEBB/The Herb Doctor,/And Medicine Man,/All Medicine/made from Indian/Herbs, Will cure/when others Fail." "*Gee!* It's GREAT/ to be an AMERICAN," states a flag-bearing sign in the window of a dry-cleaning store in Covington, Kentucky, photographed by John Vachon in September 1939, and the date is crucial: the war had just begun in Europe; "The Arming of America" was still two years away (see p. 17). The photo catches an elderly male passerby as he turns to admire the sign; the slight smile on his face seems to say, "That's how I think!" Mr. F. S. Wolcott's attitude toward his country was projected on the exterior wall of Spencer's Service Station in Port Gibson, Mississippi, in the form of a huge painted facsimile copy of President Roosevelt's 1933 typewritten thank-you letter to him, acknowledging the receipt of a "Cedar Chair . . . I have been interested in what you tell me of its construction." Documenting a document, and the shared pride of a small community, Marion Post Wolcott (no relation) photographed the gas station's mural-letter in 1939. It's grander than any official mural.

Whatever remained unsaid in a photo could always be explained in a text or caption, depending on the format of the publication. Although the discursive procedures of photojournalism are now out of favor, they were once readily accepted by documentary photographers as artful as Berenice Abbott, whose *Changing New York* (1939) was shot mainly in 1936, the year *Life* magazine first appeared. Commissioned by the Federal Art Project of the Works Progress Administration, Abbott approached the city in a neutral and straightforward manner quite apart from the elegiac stance of Walker Evans, another conservator of threatened buildings. "LYRIC THEATRE, 100 Third Avenue, Manhattan; April 24, 1936. Built about 1880. Present facade designed by George McCabe, architect, in 1910," reads the caption beneath this photo

(left) in *Changing New York*. The Beaux-Arts filigree is redolent of 1916, when the Chaplin film would have been in its first run, the Lyric's architecture and lamps extending a classy invitation each night to the tired working-class residents of the neighborhood, many of them immigrants. Only the uniform Art Deco design of the placards suggests immediately that the 1936 Lyric has kept up with the times. Chaplin is apposite because the Little Tramp's fragile hold on dignity and decorum bespeaks the theater's condition and low status here. For a more concrete description of its circumstances, however, we should quote the text by Elizabeth McCausland that supplemented the picture in the original edition: "Fifty years ago this was the Sans Souci Concert Hall where Richard Croker had a private box. Today the Lyric Theatre offers transients, seafaring men, sightseers, slummers, visual fare of two features, newsreel and a 'short'—all for ten cents. The doors open as early as 7 A.M., though the show does not start till eight; and patrons who did not have thirty cents for a night's lodging in a Bowery 'hotel' can make up their sleep." The unremarkable last clause quietly underscores a frustrating truth about photography, where omniscience is hardly a given. One good sign in a picture is worth a thousand words, at least.

The richly connotative signs in the photographs of Lange, Shahn, Post Wolcott, et al., which aspire to narrative, are different from those in the work of Walker Evans, whose signs are typically denotative, and noteworthy as lyrical and humorous objects rather than sociological observations.

By 1946, standardized commercial signs dominated small towns everywhere—as in Russell Lee's view of Welch, p. 48—but ten years earlier, in Alabama, Walker Evans could photograph this Art Deco Coca-Cola sign (right), an example of commerce humanized. Art Deco had been chic for about ten years, starting in 1926, and was in decline by the time this photo was taken; it would leave its mark on office buildings, neighborhood movie houses such as the Bay, national chain stores, and more modest outposts along obscure roads. The River Hill Cafe at once supports a common Art Deco triptych form (see next page) and a dialectic on the rule of fashion. Where the cafe's name is skillfully lettered in the Style Moderne manner, the architecture of the place can only manage to realize partially the stepped design typical of Deco buildings. The hand-painted wings of the sign, however, reject the inflected lines of the reigning style in favor of a quirky ornamentation that is surely personal, as opposed to the manufactured intimacy of Coca-Cola's cursive typeface.

Although spider webs may not rank high on every scale of values, Evans often enough photographed sanguine evidence of a vital populist humanism: signs that at once enhance the environment and provide an outlet for individual self-expression. Not satisfied with the imposing but utilitarian HORSES and MARES printed on his stable in Vicksburg, Miss., the owner adorned it with a framed painting of two affectionate horses, one black, the other white, rendered with more affection than anatomical accuracy. Like many of the decorative scenes and devices included in these signs, it is a good example of American folk art. In South Carolina, Evans found and photographed a compact display of signs on a porch: ART SCHOOL, PUBLIC/STENOGRAPHER, FISH CO., and FRUITS/VEGETABLES, the latter featuring a lovely still life of free-floating produce quite innocent of depth, perspective, and gravity. A stranger to schools of art everywhere, the painter has nonetheless signed his work in the corner, as any self-respecting artist would. In Baton Rouge, Louisiana, Evans took a tight close-up of a singular landscape painted on a dry-cleaning store by the Magritte of the local limners: spiffy jacket, white shirt and tie mounted on a stick and flanked evenly by two stylized saplings. This fundamental impulse toward balance, symmetry, and order is documented in most of Evans's sign pictures. All hands seem to partake of it, however unconsciously. There are no less than sixteen informational signs on the River Hill Cafe, yet everything is in the right place. The front wall of the Cherokee Parts Store and Garage in Atlanta, Georgia, is festooned with an array of tires, inner tubes, and hubcaps that combine to form a perfect field of visual harmony and felicity, the comic strip *Gasoline Alley* by way of Mondrian. Imagine that these scenes were culled from the same neighborhood, bordering Main Street; who wouldn't want to live there? (See *Walker Evans: First and Last* [1978], pp. 95, 69, 68, and 97, respectively.) But these walls and painted signs are made of wood, a most vulnerable material. Caught in time, the River Hill Cafe stands cheerfully for its picture, its plight notwithstanding. The left side of the building, a list-

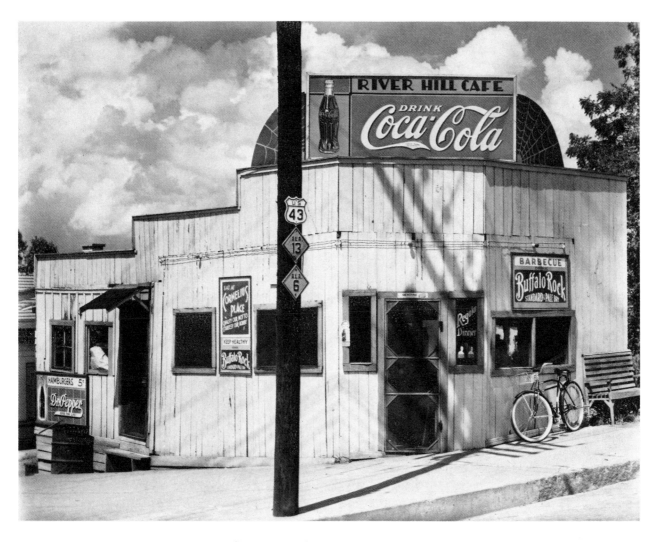

Walker Evans, *Roadside Restaurant, Alabama, 1936.*

ing or slowly sinking ship, threatens the stability defined spatially by the telephone pole and the sign, a
grand bannerlike emblem, thanks to the compositional exactitude of Evans, adept of Flaubert and
Baudelaire. Because the presence of people would
compromise the transcendent quality of this scene,
the bicycle must stand for the multitude of children

who once gathered here after school, or before the
picture show on Saturdays.

Evans's way with an old building has left its mark
on the photographs of George Tice, whose *Urban
Landscapes* (1975) seem divided between the Evans
tack (p. 69) and the less evocative approach of a
Berenice Abbott (the Tice photo on p. 61).

Whatever George Tice intended to express or document when he photographed this theater in 1974 (right), any viewer with a strong sense of the thirties is bound to respond to the ideals of style and idea of transport formulated here by several international signs. This movie theater opened on Albany Street, New Brunswick, New Jersey, in 1937. Its curved contours, bands of lines, and glazed terra-cotta tiles were principal features of the last phase of Art Deco, which is variously called Style Moderne, Streamlined Moderne, or Depression Modern. Although the streamlined style was hardly monolithic, it dominated its own decade as no single style has since the turn of the century. Throughout the thirties, aerodynamic imagery and form shaped an astonishing range of objects and products, from pencil sharpeners and vacuum cleaners to gas stations and of course the "China Clipper" airship, as though sleek design could somehow collectively carry an entire nation out of the Great Depression. A young New Jersey stenographer might well have begun her day in 1937 by opening a box of Elizabeth Arden or Jacqueline Cochran makeup (named after the aviatress), either package comprising a veritable miniature of Albany Street's International Cinema, black base topped by white walls, the order of the day, hers in particular: a morning cup of coffee at the bright new White Tower restaurant; lunch at the Horn & Hardart Automat; a stroll through the auto showroom exhibiting next year's Cord or Lincoln Zephyr; and, later, after a tiring afternoon taking dictation, a stop at the local branch of Cushman's Bake Shop, and,

after dinner, the double feature at the International: Humphrey Bogart as a pilot in *China Clipper* ("Rough air! Wind! Rain! Lightning! We're flying by instruments!" he radios Pat O'Brien back at the base) and Ginger Rogers and Fred Astaire in *Shall We Dance?,* set on a dazzlingly white ocean liner. Its stylized portholes were a standard device in Style Moderne architecture, right down to *Pluto's Dream House,* an animated cartoon from 1940, the year that America sailed out of the Depression and into the full employment occasioned by World War II. "BOOM TOWN" declares the flag-bedecked Style Moderne marquee of a theater, photographed for the FSA by Jack Delano during a Labor Day parade in 1940.

Was the tonic effect of a *Shall We Dance?* predicated at all on the way its totally Art Deco "look" cohered with and extended the Moderne components of the audience's environment? Certainly the International Cinema theater reminded everyone of an ocean liner. It must be said, however, that even in its prime, the smokestack must have looked a bit gauche and out of place, like a very short fellow trying to call attention to himself at a cocktail party. Did anyone think this way on Albany Street in the thirties, or were they too naive, too set on transportation to make such judgments? "Shall we dance/Or keep on moping?" sings Fred Astaire, who was built to sail through space as smoothly and rapidly as possible. The same cannot be said of the smokestack, which owes something to the Bauhaus-inspired International Style, progenitor of contemporary glass-

George Tice, *The New International Cinema, Albany Street, New Brunswick, New Jersey, February 1974.*

walled cities. The smokestack is architecturally wrong for its space, and badly designed. It should be angled back, if only as a figurative defense against the winds of change. The tenement overshadows the cinema, just as television and the austere International Style would by the late nineteen-forties overwhelm motion pictures and all vestiges of the soft-contoured Style Moderne. Renovated inside with delicatessen pasteboard, the "New" version of this movie house features *That Man Bolt,* an international Kung Fu thriller that had better attract audiences or the theater will soon sink or return to drydock for one last repair.

In 1954, when Dorothea Lange shot the Dixie Auto-Vu in St. George, Utah (right), moviegoing was in a slump, along with documentary photography. Veterans of the thirties such as Lange were now spending a good deal of their time photographing distant places (Ireland and Burma) or the trees in their own backyards, possibly because the problems engendered by American prosperity seemed to defy old documentary approaches, particularly the assumption that a sign or two could gloss the life in a picture. Given the intuitive procedures of most photographers, Lange probably never said as much, but it is easy to see that she seldom again aimed her camera at signs as she once had. "All signs point to FORD V-8," declares an Alabama billboard in a Lange photo from 1936. The car in the ad speeds into the future, its optimism and velocity ironically counterpointed in the foreground by an ox-drawn wagon that is being driven by an old black man. Reprinted again and again, it is a "classic" FSA shot, as is Lange's 1939 photo of two satchel-bearing farm workers trudging along a highway in California, past a billboard advising them to RELAX and NEXT TIME TRY THE TRAIN. Such juxtapositions challenge the laws of probability, like some of Cartier-Bresson's great chance shots from the thirties (a man leaping across a puddle in tandem with a dancer's leap on a poster behind him [Paris, 1932]) or the more corrosive images he made in the American manner during his first tour of this country in 1946–47 (e.g. an automobile graveyard in Tennessee marked by a large wooden roadside cross reading JESUS IS COMING SOON). Of course Lange did not want her viewers to take delight in such pictures and their nascent metaphysics of Surreal coincidence. She only wanted to communicate a message: advertising as the principal discourse of capitalist culture? "We are two nations"? It seems too simple now. Many signs do indeed lend themselves to easy ironies and reductive messages; all signs do not point to Ford, or heartless capitalism, even in Lange. If the entire archive of FSA photographs has a collective hero, it is the resilient spirit of the American small town. Its signs of life, the heartbeat of the nation, are rarely present in Lange's solemn if not hopeless pictures of the American fifties.

Although the plastic signs on St. George's Dixie Auto-Vu are potentially quite funny (tight close-up of signs against mountains and mesas: Utah as Dixie? Peter Pan above the desert? How good is your vu?), Lange chose an angle of vision which minimizes the words and presents the overhead wires and drive-in as a threat to nature. Her foreground view of the expanse of earth and gravel aggravated by tires anticipates by two decades the "environmentalist" landscape photographers of the new West, including Robert Adams, Frank Gohlke, Joel Sternfeld, and Lewis Baltz (the latter specializes in atrocity shots of mounds of earth and empty plots that have been recently ravaged by bulldozers and tractors). The population of St. George, it turns out now, suffers from a high incidence of cancer, the result, it seems, of radioactive fallout from atomic bomb tests of the early nineteen-fifties. The Auto-Vu's screen is a wretched patchwork quilt, and we ought to

Dorothea Lange, *St. George, Utah, 1954.*

pity the audience, though Lange herself is not interested in drive-in moviegoing per se, or the idea of each car as an isolation booth, a sad substitute for a theater or some other stone-solid communal place. Her young friend Robert Frank, however, would soon respond to this aspect of the American road, and lead photographers away from signs and data, toward a more subjective kind of documentary photography (as on p. 31). Diane Arbus points to the end of this road; her work of the nineteen-sixties virtually closes the book on signs of the

thirties. Except for her version of a Grosz cartoon—an odd-looking fellow wearing a pro-[Vietnam]war button—Arbus avoids words altogether, which is photographically pure and good, since all but the best sign-bearing pictures should remind us that photos do not explain things very well. The end of the road is marked by Chauncey Hare, who uses a wide-angle lens instead of words to emphasize the totally depressed state of his *Interior America* (1978), where no one goes out to the movies and even the blank TV screens look sad.

Moviegoing is just another dead-end in Robert Frank's *The Americans,* whose collected photographs of the mid nineteen-fifties seem to transform social observations into a sustained subjective response, signs included. His pictures are so consistent in mood that one comes to feel the presence of the photographer, as though he were the quietly despairing narrator of a novel such as Walker Percy's *The Moviegoer* (1961). Set in and around New Orleans in 1957, the year after Frank photographed this Detroit drive-in (right), *The Moviegoer* is narrated by a young man named Binx who hopes to break out of "the everydayness of his life" and face the implications of several events, including his near-death in Korea. After watching the Mardi Gras parade briefly, Binx and his companion Kate escape the crowds and go to a movie: "*Panic in the Streets* with Richard Widmark is playing [nearby]. The movie was filmed in New Orleans . . . Widmark is a public health inspector who learns that a culture of cholera bacilli has gotten loose in the city," says Binx, whose creator has Camus's *Plague* (1947) on his mind. Kate, Binx's friend, is gripped by a scene in the film which shows the very neighborhood of the theater. After the show, she looks around the neighborhood, and says, "Yes, it is certified now." To Binx, movies certify most everything. He is happy at any picture, good or bad. He even savors drive-ins and would no doubt enjoy himself at the *Outdoor Theater and Cheyenne Mountain* photographed in 1968 by Robert Adams (overleaf, left), who in the nineteen-seventies led a movement away from the wide-angled dynamism of Frank, toward a highly descriptive, dispassionate, and often elegant perusal of environmental clutter and chaos. Although Adams expresses his hatred of suburban sprawl in his Preface to *The New West* (1974), the standardized signs in his paradoxical photos are succinct and unpromising denotative tags such as GAS, allowing the brilliant sunlight to glow unashamedly in each jerry-built place. His images rarely try to talk or editorialize, which cannot be said of *The Americans.* A handful of its pictures identify Frank as the last FSA photographer, as in the close-up of a pinball machine backed by a row of campaign posters, with STATE TREASURER at the center. But other signs in *The Americans* point to a malaise or illness which has spread beyond the body politic, as in the photo of a shell-shocked Jehovah's Witness who is selling copies of *AWAKE!,* the sort of gritty image Louis Faurer was regularly producing in the late forties, when he shared a darkroom with Frank, whom he surely influenced. "EDGE OF DOOM," proclaims a Times Square marquee in a photo of Faurer's from 1949, in which all the pedestrians are walking in the same direction, like pod-people at the end of *Invasion of the Body Snatchers* (1956), spellbound denizens of the Age of Conformity who have heard the Word. Frank snapped it more than once. A large sign above five old gas pumps in a deserted service station in Santa Fe exhorts us to SAVE—our souls, of course, not gas. To Frank, we are all installed or stalled here, under that sign or in this drive-in, marking time: a sunset blocked by a drive-in screen, a movie compromised by twilight; what's the difference, who cares, is there any-

Robert Frank, *Drive-in, Detroit,* 1956.

Robert Adams, *Outdoor Theater and Cheyenne Mountain,* 1968.

Bruce Davidson, *Sub-division, Daly City, California,* 1965.

thing else to do but "flick-out"? The cars are jammed in, there's no exit in view. Dorothea Lange's glum but open highway has been closed for the Cold War. Stephen Shore's Bay Theatre and Russell Lee's fluid and optimistic postwar Main Street are truly out of the picture. The sign atop Frank's screen is illegible, thankfully, for a comprehensible word might impose a gratuitous or heavy irony. The sky is heavy enough already, and, typical of Frank, its grainy and gray texture—a graphic fall-out, the sign of this *auteur*—is equivalent to the sense of alienation and anomie evident throughout *The Americans,* where the sun rarely breaks through. Bruce Davidson agrees with Frank: these screens certify nothing (above). His 1965 photograph of a Western subdivison and drive-in is direct and unambiguous, as statements often were in those days. He needs no words to help him posit the new neighborhood as a graveyard, its residents done in by the bleak tonalities and thick, heavy air of an exhaust fumes and A-bomb culture.

Sunday evening was "Family Night" at the Play-house Theatre (1922–) and many other neighbor-hood movie houses during the nineteen-forties: tickets at a discount, children seated grandly with their parents in the middle of the theater instead of the kiddie section, and then you'd have a soda and sand-wich after the show, and a chance to discuss the main feature with your folks, and replay the best scenes, and be too excited to sleep when you got home. The old theaters are in poor health now, along with their neighborhoods; and many have gone out of business or disappeared entirely, like the Temple and the In-ternational, the Lyric and the Paradise—paradise lost, one is tempted to say. The pious and elegiac tone may well set some teeth on edge here, especially if one doesn't object to the ambience at shopping center cinemas, no neighborhood in sight, or be-lieve that the activities along Main Street on a Satur-day or Sunday were part of a precious communality.

My own sense of moviegoing and photography has been determined or sharpened by the circumstances and dictates of illness. At the age of forty-two, at the end of the July 4, 1976, Bicentennial weekend, which had been spent at home, watching on TV the tall ships cavorting in New York harbor—a thrilling, ephem-eral sight—I suffered a massive and quite unex-pected heart attack, a Pearl Harbor in me, as I soon came to call it. During a long and stressful period of recovery and readjustment, my helpful memory per-formed all sorts of miracles, creating a seemingly im-perishable Williamsburg of the mind by restoring lost interiors and facades. At night, however, they often turned out to be even more vulnerable than the structures in a photograph by Walker Evans. Home in my own bed after a month in the hospital, I dreamed that I was back in the town of my youth (1940 pop-ulation: 11,000), at the Playhouse on Family Night, my future wife and children somehow seated beside me, watching the forest fire scene in *Bambi* (1942), the flames leaping higher and higher—too high! [col-lective gasp]—they've left the screen, igniting the curtains, the Playhouse is burning, flames are shoot-ing from the Moorish battlements above the screen, people are screaming and running toward the side doors, but they won't open, they're jammed, there's no air, and I wake up, drenched by perspiration. On a subsequent night I dreamed that I was walking alone to the Playhouse to catch the early show on a warm Sunday evening. It was dusk, and the street-lamps were lit discreetly at their wartime level; no enemy bombers would ever find Long Island. I stopped short on the tree-lined side street by the theater because one of its exit doors had been left open. What luck! I glanced to the right to see if there was a cop on the busy corner or any grown-up who might recognize me. The coast was clear, so I stepped quickly into the darkened Playhouse. Cinders and rubble stir and crumble underfoot. It's all burnt-out—a cavern. I remember the fire—it wasn't a dream!—and rush back into the street again. All the lights are now out, the cars and trees and people have disappeared, there is no neighborhood, only absolute darkness, mat black. Are my eyes open or closed? My stomach sinks. I am stranded, or Stranded, to

George Tice, *Strand Theatre, Front Street, Keyport, New Jersey, September 1973.*

use the sign in the above photo quite arbitrarily to install myself in George Tice's dusky picture, *Strand Theatre, Front Street, Keyport, New Jersey,* photographed in September 1973, in his best Walker Evans manner. "Are you Catholic?" a tactless nurse or attendant had asked when the paramedics deposited me in the emergency room. "No." I should have answered, "No, I'm on my own, it's up to me, my mind is open." What is the prognosis for the Strand, based on the evidence in this picture? Will it survive, like the Bay, also photographed in 1973? Its advanced age is against it, it's missing several bulbs, and a native of Kansas or Oklahoma might say that the front wall is illumined by tornado light. Watch out! But at least the marquee is on, a hopeful sign, particularly if this is the early show on a Monday evening.

IN THE DARK

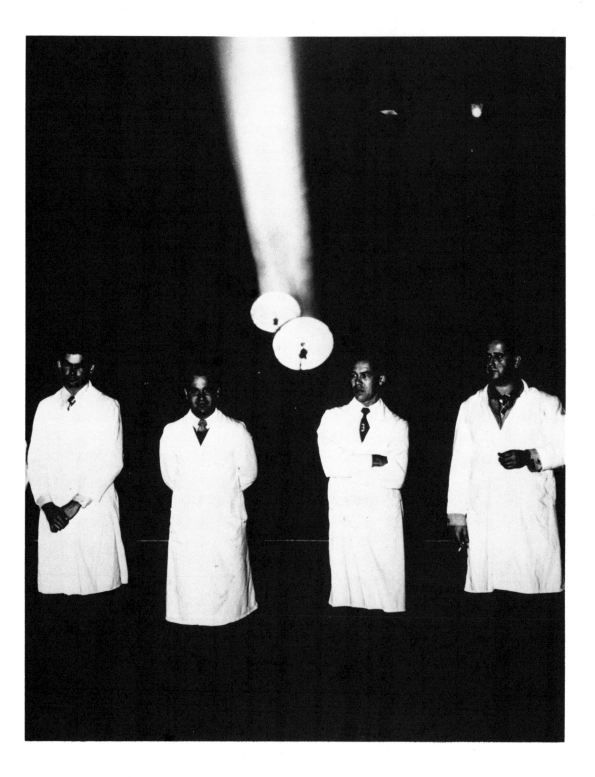

In the Dark

Everyone is an expert, a potential theorist of popular culture, and why not? Each generation of children and adolescents shares a more or less common pop experience or existence, and though some of us keep up with the times better than others, we are ready with an opinion if, say, the subject of "Television Violence and the Future of Mankind" comes up for discussion at a party; after all, we've had a democratic upbringing, and we did or did not become a sex fiend or join the Marines because of the movies and *Life* magazine. Yet we are more in the dark about such matters than we want to know or admit, since our grasp of a movie or any kind of popular image isn't necessarily any more acute than our perception of a larger reality. Before we decide whether an image is "good" or "bad" in one way or another, shouldn't we see how well we agree about what we have seen there?

What do we have here, for instance? The photographer's flashgun has amputated the legs of these men (left) by cancelling all intermediary tones between harshest black and white, producing a surreal and spectral image. The occasion is a Hollywood premiere in about the year 1950, the only solid information available on the photo, which was taken by [identity withheld because his strong personality would possibly color the response of anyone familiar with his work]. Who are these four white-coated men and why are they here? No one knows, but our guesses may shed some light on basic problems. Fifteen friends and colleagues were invited to take a stab in the dark, as in the doubloon chapter of *Moby-Dick*. They were informed only that their ambiguous coin was struck at a Hollywood movie premiere. Three people voted for "butchers," two for "lab technicians," and one each for "klieg-light operators," "Rolls-Royce chauffeurs," "caterers," "factory workers on a break," "Klansmen without hoods," "doctors," "interns," and "coroners." The editor of the standard edition of *Moby-Dick* identified them as "whale butchers." One frivolous answer was disallowed ("Halloween trick-or-treaters"). No prizes were given. The leader of the group chose "ambulance drivers," in part because Nathanael West has determined, in *The Day of the Locust,* that movies and apocalyptic movie premieres are dangerous to your health. What's wrong with the man on the left? Is he asleep on his feet, like a combat-weary soldier? He's probably blinking at the camera's flash, the only certain illumination on him, but still, we want to know more; words never hurt a picture. The interrogative mode will be indulged here. This photograph? Weegee took it—around the time of his *Naked Hollywood* (1953), with its Westian movie premieres—and Weegee's name alone darkens the picture. Without such knowledge, the words "amputate" and "harshest" might not have been ascribed to the image.

Weegee, *Palace Theatre, New York City,* 1945.

Weegee wanted to penetrate the darkness, quite literally, as in this photo, *Palace Theatre, New York City, 1945* (above), which can serve as a companion to his picture of the four white-coated men. At the center of the photo, and of central interest to Weegee if not to us, is a passionate couple, their privacy violated by Weegee's infrared approach. This is lighter-spirited and less compromising than other such findings by Weegee the nighthawk and shameless voyeur, the Weegee best summarized by his *Naked City* photo of a lone woman who is seated in the dark atop a Life Guard Station at Coney Island, biting her fingernails as she stares at the sea or at the lovers in action on the beach—off-camera, unfortunately. "It was after midnight and jet black. One of those nights when the moon forgets to come out," writes Weegee in *Naked City,* prefacing a sequence of beach photos, his prose echoing the manner of Raymond Chandler, a kindred soul (the tough/sentimental nexus). We may resist the voyeuristic aspects of Weegee because his guilt-free camera of the nineteen-forties so clearly bespeaks our own X-rated curiosities as man and boy. Thank God for photography and *National Geographic* magazine, which allowed us, as children, to look at naked Samoan breasts and the inside of a crowded igloo. How many dared to imagine the nocturnal perspectives enjoyed by sleepless and wide-eyed Eskimo children? A Payne Fund social scientist might have offered the scene before us as additional evidence that movies inspire immorality. Weegee's woman has obviously shed her coat with reckless haste. Hot stuff on the screen!—though you wouldn't know it from the demeanor of the others here. The range of their expressions is in fact bewildering; Weegee seems to have recorded reactions to several different screen actions. Are they watching a comedy? Or newsreel footage of the fire-bombing of Japan, or coverage of a bloody urban disaster, the sort Weegee often shot, bystanders laughing as well as crying? Hysterical monists should proceed to their shelters in an orderly fashion. The smiling faces in the Palace are contradicted by the indifferent, bored, and dazed expressions of several others seated there, particularly those clustered in the two rows, top left,

which may well be an outing of retarded people, the eventual domain of Diane Arbus, Weegee's most fervent admirer among contemporary photographers. The closed expressions on many of these faces help to define social and psychological polarities and the different kinds of information one hopes to elicit from a photograph. All but one of the men here wear ties and jackets, reminding us that moviegoing was once a considerable occasion, and that life in public was more formal if not more decorous and hence "better." The family at the top right of the photo, possibly its most private juncture, seems to be concentrating more intensely than the others. If this is so, it may be because they are by comparison an isolated trio, their view of the screen free from obstructing heads, their perceptions less mediated or affected by the reactions of neighbors. Seated in the dark, alone—and remember, it is *dark* here—the dreamy member of an audience recognizes his fantasies and feelings up there, on the screen, where *other* people can also see them, but he shouldn't worry, they're probably not seeing quite the same thing as he. In Carlos Fuentes's novel *Holy Place* (1969), an aging film star is asked by a journalist, "What is a good movie?" "The one the spectator thinks he dreamed when he's leaving the theater," she answers, phrasing a commonplace cleverly. Indeed, because of Weegee's vantage point above their eyelids, many of his theater subjects appear to be sleeping. And one of the happiest, in dark glasses, lower left, may be blind, a theorist of mass culture who has seen nothing here to make her change her mind.

Aaron Siskind, *Sleeping with White Pin-ups,* 1940.

A photograph is a secret about a secret," said Diane Arbus. The subject of Aaron Siskind's photo *Sleeping with White Pin-ups* (above) may or may not be equivalent to the Arab police Captain in the movie *Beat the Devil* (1954), a grotesque who lives in a room papered with female pin-ups, Rita Hayworth foremost. Although this fellow's more balanced wall includes (left to right) Edward G. Robinson, Dolores Del Rio, James Stewart, Ingrid Bergman, Joan Davis, and Robert Taylor, movies were of little interest to Siskind. "The photograph was made as part of a study that followed the Harlem Document work— 1940—a study of what we understood to be 'the most crowded block in the world'—a block (if I remember correctly) that was bounded by 142 and 143 Sts. and Seventh and Lenox Aves. The man on the bed was the janitor in that house" (letter from A.S., 1977). In *Miss Lonelyhearts* (1933), West treats his more austere urban lodger to a mock-pastoral respite in the country. On his return drive, however, he is overwhelmed by misery as soon as his car reaches the crowded slums: "He saw a man who appeared to be on the verge of death stagger into a movie theater that was showing a picture called *Blonde Beauty*. . . . Men have always fought their misery with dreams," he thinks, powerful dreams "made puerile" by mass culture. But what if *Blonde Beauty* revived that man? And does this janitor's crowded wall point to restorative reveries? West's authorial voice, judgmental and definitive, never allows that such possibilities exist. In *The Day of the Locust* (1939), Faye Greener's room is decorated with a large photo of Tarzan. "It showed a beautiful young man with magnificent muscles, wearing only a narrow loin cloth, who was evidently squeezing a slim girl in a tan riding habit. They stood in a jungle clearing and all around the pair writhed great vines loaded with fat orchids." It only serves to inspire Faye to "manufacture another dream," an idea for a money-making scenario almost too trite for words; West uses indirect discourse. The four movie-infused novels of Manuel Puig eschew omniscience and oppose West's cold outside view with interior perspectives made possible by occluded narratives. Puig's self-contained spaces are arranged like warrens in a tenement shorn of its protective front wall—a bevy of Siskind sleepers each supplied with a comic strip thought-balloon. These first-person monologues, letters, diaries, term papers, and unmediated conversations are informed everywhere by a popular culture which is just that, a culture, an anthropological given which is as interesting and insipid, refreshing and depressing, revelatory and mysterious as the stuff of dreams. Constellations of movie stars brighten and illuminate many of these lonely chambers, though one of Puig's female gossips complains, "I never know what she's thinking!" Life is sometimes like that, and so are photographs. Is Siskind's sleeper dreaming of Dolores Del Rio, and the Ku Klux Klan be damned? Has he assumed the identity of Robinson or Taylor? Or kept his own but borrowed one of their cars and some clothes? Comedian Richard Pryor told a 1977 interviewer that his boyhood screen favorite in the forties was Little Beaver, in the Red Ryder Westerns. "I never thought to myself, 'Little Beaver's white.' I didn't think about color—just feelings," says Pryor. In Harlem, about 1960, the audience at a Tarzan movie cheered him on as he triumphed over a tribe of renegade Africans, which seemed surprising then, but not now, as one recalls the theories of Frantz Fanon, or, more immediately, the pin-up photos of Joe Louis as well as Joe DiMaggio which dominated our wall in the forties. Everyone likes to identify with an established winner, though the precise nature of a hero's appeal is always open to question, and may remain secret. Tarzan's suggestive vines are more loaded than Faye Greener could ever imagine.

Beauty is in the eye of the beholder and his current psychoanalyst, but how many aging fellows are ready to stand up and admit that they once thrilled to the king of the jungle pictured here? "You know," says one of the movie-obsessed characters in Cabrera Infante's novel, *Three Trapped Tigers* (1965), "Códac, the Photographer of the Stars, was right. In every actor there's an actress struggling to get out." George Hurrell, chief portrait photographer at M-G-M, suggested as much in 1933 with his publicity shot of Johnny Weissmuller (right). This limp-ankled Tarzan partakes of a definite strain in the Hollywood publicity genre (1928–52) whereby hopelessly heterosexual actors such as Weissmuller, Joel McCrea, and even Bogart were made or found to look remarkably "sensitive" and "feminine." This possibly naïve convention culminates in Robert Mapplethorpe's presentation of a female body-building champion, *Lady: Lisa Lyon* (1983)—the ultimate photographic sex-role game—and looks back to *Vanity Fair* celebrity photographers of the 1920s, such as Nickolas Muray and James Abbé, who in 1922 posed a bare-chested young Jack Dempsey in tights, turning him into a *premier danseur* of the Ballets Russes, the worst defeat of his life. If the jungle in the Tarzan films is as fake as the blatantly artificial studio prop, then one may also suppose that "masculinity" is an attribute as calculated, suspect, and illusory as any other cosmetic ploy. Hurrell's still might well have illustrated an article in a fan magazine: "*Photoplay* reveals Tarzan's Beauty Tips for Teens" ("Vaseline is best for a soulful spit-curl"; "I shave my body with Schick";

"When you've got someone's eye, suck in your tummy and count to five"). Like a Polaroid snapshot taken at the annual class picnic, Hurrell describes by chance the most self-conscious creature on earth, the adolescent boy: so much to discover and prove, and words won't do, even if he had them. The inarticulate Tarzan is a representative and enviable figure because gesture suffices for him. This is how the garden variety teenaged narcissist in the early fifties used to flex his biceps when he was casually sprawled on a beach blanket, posing for everyone and no one. Has Hurrell distilled here an undercurrent in the Tarzan films which addressed at least the ambivalent and inchoate sexual yearnings of early adolescence? How many of the middle-class youths who saw *The Warriors* three or four times were drawn back to this dreamy urban fantasia, the surprise hit of 1979, because its principal street gang, leather vests against glistening bare chests, strongly suggest homosexual "rough trade"? Did my friends and I avoid the *Tarzan* comic strip when we were twelve or so because of an instinctive recoil, a sexual taboo? It was drawn by Burne Hogarth, a brilliant draftsman, and we valued such skill, collecting *Terry and the Pirates* and *Jungle Jim* to use as models for our own action drawings. But you wouldn't catch Tarzan in our rooms. As drawn by Hogarth, the comic strip's male cast extends Hurrell's vision of Tarzan, so many bodies beautiful parading on the beach at Santa Monica or poised like models in those arty photos that used to be sold under the "Classical Male Nude" rubric, fig leaves to the wind. The Tarzan movies were considerably less

George Hurrell, *Johnny Weissmuller*, 1933.

"sexy" by this time, the mid-forties. His G-string had metamorphosed into baggy suede BVDs, and middle-aged Weissmuller had become flabby and more talkative, alas. Today's viewers are always startled to discover the polymorphous sexuality of the early films: Tarzan gamboling with a potential harem of apes, *luxe, calme, et volupté;* Tarzan caressing his luxuriant mane while he rides an elephant, bareback, *comme toujours;* Tarzan atop a rampaging rhino, hugging its neck while he stabs its shank, again and again; Tarzan rolling on the ground with a bloodied lion, their posture akin to the wrestlers—or are they lovers?—in several ferocious paintings by Francis Bacon. In *Tarzan and His Mate* (1934), he defeats a romantic rival, kisses Jane, and night dissolves into dawn, which reveals Tarzan prone, above Jane. He stands, and returns his knife to its sheath. The symbolism of the languid blade in Hurrell's glamour photo is too melancholy for words. "My gun is bigger than yours!" Bogart tells master-spy Sydney Greenstreet in *Across the Pacific* (1942), speaking for Everyman—as adolescent, at least.

This war tableau (right), starring the white-helmeted androgyne on the left, elicits wonder and several questions having to do with the political and moral implications of photographic style and beauty. The photo is from *Steichen at War* (1981), a 200-picture distillation of the vast documentary/public relations file amassed by the nine-man Naval Aviation Photographic Unit directed by Edward Steichen during World War II. Taken by Steichen himself in 1943, the photo shows crewmen dragging a plane grounded by a flat tire down the flight deck of the U.S.S. *Lexington* to make room for another plane to land. Typical of Steichen's twenty-five entries in the book, it is an amazingly consistent extension of his studio manner, challenging Susan Sontag's unanswered assertion that the styles of even the greatest photographers fail to survive a change in subject matter. The crewman on the left is as graceful and dramatic as Nazimova or Katherine Cornell in Steichen's studio, or Thérèse Duncan on the Acropolis. Working in the manner of the modernists who began, in the nineteen-twenties, to poeticize and idealize the machine, Steichen and his unit could make a flattop's stationary airplanes and anti-aircraft guns look as elegant as any lathe ever photographed by Paul Strand or painted by Léger. Shot from high above the clouds, flotillas of ships seem to imitate the patterns formed by flights of migrating geese. The airborne planes in *Steichen at War* skirt cloud banks as sensual and sumptuous as those photographed by James Wong Howe for *Air Force*, Warner Bros.'s B-17 epic of 1943. Steichen's crewmen could be responding here to the shouts of

a director at the dress rehearsal of their stage version of Marc Blitzstein's *The Airborne Symphony* (1943) or some other government-sponsored hymn or love song in praise of deadly force. The white-helmeted figure and his third hand reinforce the thrust of the message by treating the machine guns to a polymorphic massage, in broad daylight, no less. Imagine Weegee here. An erotica of weaponry brings to mind Marinetti's 1935 manifesto on Italy's war with Ethiopia. "War is beautiful because it initiates the dreamt-of metalization of the human body," he wrote. "War is beautiful because it combines the gunfire, the cannonades, the cease-fire, the scents, and the stench of putrefaction into a symphony. War is beautiful because it creates new architecture, like that of the big tanks, the geometrical formation flights, the smoke spirals from burning villages, and many others." A year later, Walter Benjamin glossed this by saying that mankind's "self-alienation has reached such a degree that it can experience its own destruction as an aesthetic pleasure of the first order. This is the situation of politics which Fascism is rendering artistic." Steichen was no fascist, of course, and most of his war photos were of men rather than machines. If this photo were a play or painting, a man-made enterprise, the boom would come down on it, as it should on Billings's sculpted U.S.S. *North Carolina* (p. 18) and dance directors of the seventies such as Sam Peckinpah. Stanley Kubrick also succumbed to this aesthetic in *A Clockwork Orange* (1971), even though he had been able to mock it in *Dr. Strangelove* (1964), particularly at the start, when the two

Edward Steichen, *Crewmen Dragging a Plane,* 1943.

refueling bombers mate majestically in the sky above voluptuous Rubensesque clouds while "Try a Little Tenderness" plays on the soundtrack. A Bodies Beautiful approach to war is finally bad because, in conjunction with any censorship of the Buna Beach sort (p. 13), it denies an audience its chance to contemplate the harsh evidence that might serve to formulate and possibly ease its worst fears. The only dead men on Steichen's aircraft carriers are enclosed in expressionless canvas body-bags. For a displaced version of the carnage of war, viewers turned to *Dick Tracy,* crime movies, and Weegee's popular news photos of bloody corpses on the street, their upturned shoes sagging in opposite directions, toward the pavement, like Petroushka at rest as played by Nijinsky.

Let's play guns!'' was the loud call at the end of the school day, when we were nine and ten, around 1944, and the weather was good. We'd gather later, weapons in hand, at an inoperative golf course (there was an anti-aircraft unit on one green), and decide what kind of movie-based game it would be, War or Gangbusters, headline stuff—rarely Cowboys & Indians, which was too contrived and historically irrelevant for us. Tarzan? What a disgusting suggestion. Our props were minimal; if the game was War, "dirt bombs" could be added. Nature's hand grenades, they were chunks of hard earth found in uncultivated gardens; tossed blindly into the jungle, they might score a direct hit on a Jap sniper, as in *Guadalcanal Diary.* No illusion-shattering girls or younger siblings were allowed on the set unless we needed a nurse or medic for a big invasion. In our most expansive scenarios, each of us had a chance to play every role, to win and lose. Marine invulnerability and stoicism gave way to anguished Jap-rat histrionics. We mimed death extravagantly—staggering in slow-motion, gasping for air on the ground—and resurrection was a delightful given. The "dead" opened their eyes and sprang to their feet with a great grin when play was suspended. *"Everybody* up!"

Time may have run out for the fellows in this game (right), Spanish Harlem, about 1941, caught at the "decisive moment" by Helen Levitt, who has nothing of the clinical detachment of her hit-and-run master, Cartier-Bresson. One is reluctant to characterize or read the expression of the fellow hiding or cowering on the doorstep. Is he waiting for battle orders from the leader, or additional direction and choreography because he missed the movie they are doing? Maybe he did see it but has forgotten how *his* prototype (Muni? Robinson? Bart MacLane?) acted in this particular pinch. Or perhaps he is playing his assigned role as a coward or the first guy who runs out of ammo. The tensions recorded by Levitt suggest that the situation is grave. As a formal visual unit, the picture is nonetheless a surprisingly pleasing composition, an elegant fusion of horizontal and vertical forces whose harmonies would represent, in a perfect world, the state of mind always achieved by imitative and creative play. The steel bars, symbol and fact, allow that celluloid gunplay may not always be a satisfactory release of aggression, if that is what the action is about in this photo. Some viewers would only note that the boy in laceless shoes is as poised as a dancer, and leave it at that. Diane Arbus's *Child with a Toy Hand Grenade in Central Park, New York City, 1962* (overleaf, left) asks us to proceed with caution on all fronts. Could he be pretending that he is John Wayne or maybe Audie Murphy, the one-man army of World War II, who—dream of dreams—played himself in *To Hell and Back* (1955)? Did the boy see them on TV? Was the grenade advertised there, along with the "G.I. Joe" doll and jungle kit, a staple of the sixties? Did the boy serve in Vietnam eight years later? In *Dispatches* (1977), Michael Herr describes how zonked Nam infantrymen fought their own little self-contained cassette recorder John Wayne rock'n'roll wars. Arbus has probably caught some kind of pathology or malignancy here, one that may

Helen Levitt, *New York City,* ca. 1941.

Diane Arbus, *Child with a Toy Hand Grenade in Central Park, New York City, 1962.*

or may not have something to do with movies, TV war shows (e.g., *Combat*), or the lurid war comic books (*Sgt. Rock; Weird War Tales*) that have been consumed quietly for forty years, Vietnam notwithstanding. Does the boy want to blow up the world? or only himself and the enemy combat photogra-pher—whose own terrible tensions have drawn her to this combustible target? He's as thin as a war orphan, and not too pleased to have his picture taken. Helen Levitt would have used a right-angle viewfind-er to catch him unawares (under siege in a day-dream?). Bill Owens returns us to safer suburban

Bill Owens, *We Like to Play War,* ca. 1970.

ground in his photo of two California boys, taken about 1970 (above), which bids adieu to *Beau Geste* (p. 21), tells us to forget about dirt bombs, but don't worry, there will always be an army, even if its Boy Commandos are supplied by K Mart and distracted by the violent spectacle of pro football (note the Denver Broncos logo on the boy on the right). The terrain here has been devastated by suburban "development," there is scarcely a place to hide, and, if I were nine again, I wouldn't want to play with them. The Defense Department only wonders if such boys have been conditioned to really fight.

As the war ended and adolescence approached, we put down our guns in favor of bats and balls. Although we followed all major sports and went to every sports movie, baseball alone was an abiding, trans-seasonal pastime, offering mental giants an encyclopedic body of statistical lore that could be commanded more easily than a baseball field. History engaged us along with current events. Babe Ruth, whose wide nostrils had always made him look as though he could draw more oxygen than other men, came alive again in the picture-books and magazines which appeared after he died from cancer in 1948. The news photos of him in decline were made even more poignant by adjacent images of the Babe in his prime, when he looked ready to swab his glove with mustard and gulp it down whole. We impersonated the omnipotence of the great players, past and present, in a game of our own invention, played near home in a large, empty lot that had a back fence which served us as the outfield walls of big league ballparks of our choice, depending on the scenario. It took only two fellows to play this game, one stationed in the outfield and the other at home plate, hitting the ball himself and describing the action, play-by-play, radio-style (we'll skip the rules) as the Dodgers battled the Yankees or the National and American League All-Time All-Star Best teams squared off in a dream game ("The Bambino, the immortal Sultan of Swat, is advancing to the plate, hefting his lumber"). "Home plate" was invisible, a state of mind, adjusted at will to allow one to hit home runs more easily. If, after five minutes, no home runs had been hit, we'd move home plate closer to the fence. Rizzuto and Reese were satisfied with singles, but when DiMaggio or Ruth came to bat, the hitter always took five or six steps toward the fence before he took his mightiest swing and then watched the ball soar toward the bleachers of Yankee Stadium. The fans were allowed to walk across its cavernous outfield after a real game there in the late forties. If the boys who dashed back and forth in deepest center field imagining themselves to be DiMaggio had only stopped for a moment to look toward home plate they might have experienced a surge of panic. Where *was* home plate? A cloud of cigarette smoke hung over the far end of the field, turning the fans in the grandstand behind the home plate area into a blurred grayish mass. How in the world did DiMaggio manage to pick up the trajectory of a little ball hit out of such a miasma? How could any human being negotiate this space, and all that it stood for?

W. Eugene Smith's 1941 photo of DiMaggio (right) at once telescopes the vastness of Yankee Stadium and partially answers these questions by picturing a sports hero who is less a man than a monument. By having him look away from the camera, a clever reversal of a clichéd pose, Smith denied DiMaggio any personality or self, approximating the impression always given by "The Brown Bomber," Joe Louis, an imperturbable fighting machine. Where Ruth's nickname obviously denoted basic human appetites, DiMaggio's "Yankee Clipper" evoked another powerful airplane and, in fascist enclaves of the Bronx, Marinetti's "dreamt-of-metalization of the human

W. Eugene Smith, *Joe DiMaggio,* 1941. © 1979 Time, Inc.

body." Now that sports stars show their faces everywhere and won't stop talking, can they possibly figure in anyone's imagination as they once did? "I must have confidence and I must be worthy of the great DiMaggio who does all things perfectly even with the pain of the bone spur in his heel. What is a bone spur?" wonders Santiago as he struggles with the big fish in Hemingway's *The Old Man and the Sea* (1952). "Do you believe the great DiMaggio would stay with a fish as long as I will stay with this one? he thought." All this over Mr. Coffee? a younger reader may think.

With the advent of early adolescence, the movie-based action moved indoors, or at least it did for the white middle-class inasmuch as smoking was strictly verboten. Cigarettes were now at the center of our stage and screen. Survival kits on life-rafts included a pack, as we knew from war films, and the driven and often doomed heroes or anti-heroes of the movies we loved best—they are now called *films noirs*—could not have survived or died properly without their supplements of cigarettes. Mortally wounded, they hung on till someone proffered a smoke, from which they drew one deep, long, last drag [Tight close-up of face] and then, with their *very* last breath, they would offer us a hard-boiled wisecrack or metaphor [Music up]. As expressive and pervasive as fog in Dickens, the heavy, curling smoke emitted by tough guys of the forties drifted and spread everywhere.

The two boys in this Helen Levitt photo (right), taken about 1941, straddle two decades. Bogart as Roy Earle, the Last Gangster, scans the horizon in *High Sierra* (1941), while the self-indulgent player in the foreground does his own stuff, papa, a street cool out of Cagney, George Raft, and, on a lower level, Leo Gorcey and Huntz Hall of the Dead End Kids. The high-pockets style in pants is strictly Little Caesar (1930) as played by the actor born Emanuel Goldenberg, one more pretender. Our models and instructors in the mid and late nineteen-forties included baseball players who endorsed cigarettes—"Joe DiMaggio Smokes Chesterfields," Dixie Walker for Old Golds, Mel Ott for Camels—and actors such as Dick Powell, Alan Ladd, Fred MacMurray, Robert Mitchum, Edmond O'Brien, and, above all, Bogart, whose compulsive smoking was so inextricably part of the Bogart character. No one could equal his skill at lighting-up in bad weather, after dark, creating in his cupped hand a chiaroscuro that even now could enhance the appearance and appeal of a fellow of any age. The Romanticism of all this is clear enough. Bogart's economy of gesture and verbal expression encode the best Hemingway; his heart belongs to Raymond Chandler. Where the trenchcoat is Byronic and old-fashioned, the only soft thing about Dick Tracy or Hammett's Sam Spade, the cigarette is existential and contemporary—the Bogart-loner's most constant companion, his sole support and comfort. Yet it too would betray him, and many others as well, if the movie-inspired puffing and preening of our youth fathered the truly sickening chain-smoking of the man. At twelve, we locked ourselves in the bathroom, smoked our first unfiltered Chesterfield, felt faint—lesser men vomited—and, after many subsequent rehearsals in the mirror, learned to smile, talk, and laugh with a cigarette in our mouth, the way Bogart did, no tears from the fumes, though we were more fastidious than he in regard to telltale ashes in the sink, and cravenly waved smoke out the window—out *there,* where we should have been slouched, showing off for females—my God, where's the bottle of Air-Wick?

At sixteen, in high school, we struggled vainly to light cigarettes on one match, at night, in the rain or wind, for girls or ourselves—chiaroscuro would have

Helen Levitt, *New York City,* ca. 1941.

to come later. At college, the weed became a social prop at parties, but this mise-en-scène is too tedious to evoke. Instead, we should animate Helen Levitt's two street performers. [Scene: basement steps below their perch] "Mother of Mercy, is this the end of Little Benny?" "It curtains for me too, Benny. It gettin' *dark* in here. [Pause. Then, in a higher, excited voice:] Hey, man, Mistuh Edward G. *You*-know-who! Who supposed to light *my* smoke if we both"— but that's enough. Thirty years after my first movie-induced cigarettes, I found myself in the hospital, a reformed smoker at last.

Mary Ellen Mark's untitled 1976 photo of a mental patient (right) isn't opaque, like Weegee's premiere, but it too begs an explanation, some words. The photo was taken in the women's high-security ward of the Oregon State Hospital, where *One Flew Over the Cuckoo's Nest* had recently been filmed. The uncommonly large publicity glossy is of Michael Douglas, TV star (*The Streets of San Francisco*), movie actor, and producer of *Cuckoo's Nest*. The scarf, or security blanket, is an affecting accouterment, but still we are impatient for more information: why is this woman here, locked up, and is there a name for her malady? What did she do to land here? And what does she do here, in this cell? Of course our desire to know may point to needs as questionable as the camera's intrusion on this woman's privacy. A voyeuristic perspective usually compromises the consumer, but in this instance we're home free, no moral duty to pay, for the intimation of pathology, with its glamour image/object, has more than one equivalent in the world of the normal. The dreamy publicity pin-up is now off the wall, so to speak. It is arrayed next to her head, and ours as well, the place where anything can and does come to life, which is not only sexual. Let the glossy 8-by-10 be a metaphor as well as a partner.

Point of view and perspective function similarly. By using a wide-angle lens and the rim of the bed as a frame, the photographer created a radical foreshortening which suggests the circumstances of a dungeon at the same time that it renders the hypertrophied vision of an afflicted or tormented person.

If this poor woman were to look up, the ceiling might rise and soar as in a cathedral. How far, in fact, does the expanding universe of imagination extend? Mars? Downtown Oregon? Could the streets of San Francisco squeeze into this cell? My own hospital room turned out to be spacious. As I was lying there, very ill, staring at whiteness, astonished, cursing myself for the cigarette habit, cursing the old movies—no solace in that, I did it, me—the small windowless room suddenly swelled and expanded on three sides of the bed and my wide-angle lens perceived that the room had become a vast municipal dumping ground consisting solely of cigarette waste, hundreds of thousands of discarded smokes, piled as high as the bed and extending as far as one could see, small hills and valleys of them—there must be a million butts, dry, burnt-out, broken, twisted, contorted, shriveled, crumbling old cigarettes, some damp or sodden with coffee or Coke, such recent discharges forming dark brown patches like mounds of freshly turned earth or something much worse, a foul-smelling presence, an infinite mistake, close, stifling . . . open a window, please! I closed my eyes against it, gulped air, and remembered (in the space devoted to Michael Douglas) the deathly full-page close-up of Bogart taken by Avedon, and my panic as a child of three or four when a wave knocked me out of my father's arms in the ocean and I discovered that I couldn't breathe underwater. Someone was adjusting my oxygen mask, she looked like Ann Sheridan, a leading nurse in the movie about the nurses of Bataan. Think about nurses in old movies. Trivia. Play it. Claudette Col-

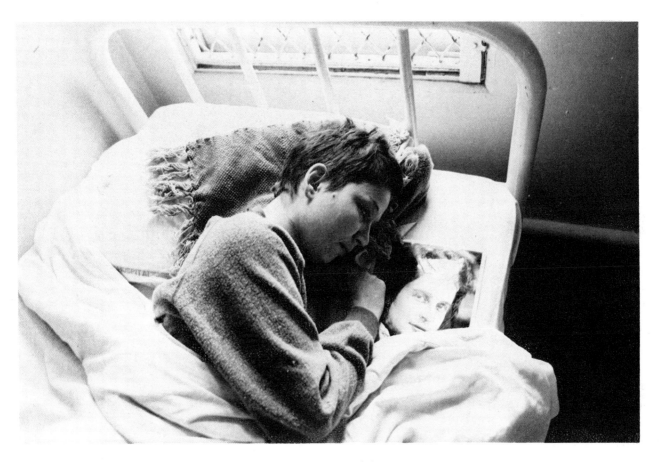

Mary Ellen Mark, Untitled, 1976.

bert. Jennifer Jones. Laraine Day in *The Story of Dr. Wassell.* 1944. The year. I took small, brief, intelligent breaths—pace yourself, pace yourself. Ann Sothern, Priscilla Something. That big mean one, Hope Emerson. Mrs. Pruneface! The Playhouse. The nurse at the foot of the bed, the doctor, my wife, my parents, they all looked eight feet tall, their faces distant, diminished by my underwater perspective. Weegee's white-coated medical men waiting in the dark are surely an unsettling sight, even if scholarship should one day unearth a caption identifying them as a team of movie makeup men ready to touch up any flawed stars before the photographers can get them.

ILLUSIONS AND TRANSFORMATIONS

Eugene Robert Richee, *Veronica Lake,* 1941.

Millions of 8-by-10-inch movie-star glossies have been distributed free to fans, newspapers, and magazines, but the old glamour genre (1925–60) compels attention even now. It has recently enjoyed a small critical renaissance, and its photographic deceptions continue to manifest fundamental yearnings. Like Karsh of Ottawa and the most modest neighborhood photo studios on Main Streets everywhere, the portrait galleries of Hollywood tried to perform a simple task: idealize the subject. Answerable to the advertising and publicity departments of their studios, the galleries were in action continuously, now and then extending their facilities to visiting photographers from *Life* magazine or fellow travelers in flattery such as Edward Steichen, who from 1923 to 1938 was chief photographer for *Vogue* and *Vanity Fair.* Although the tag "glamour portraiture" is by definition a non sequitur, a send-up of the idea of documentary truth, the genre nonetheless set standards for the public, the way photography always does in the modern world. A 1941 audience might have inferred several things from Eugene Robert Richee's photo of Veronica Lake (b. Constance Ockleman), which is far from being a masterpiece of the glamour genre (left).

The artifice of the Main Street shutterbug was even more transparent: poorly painted Arcadian backdrops instead of fabricated environments; florid poses where expert lighting would have enhanced or created the sitter's importance and distinction; radical open-face surgery on the negative to transform the patient into a prettier, handsomer, much younger person. The crudeness of such operations is all too evident, since ordinary people, unlike stars, walk in the neighborhood and receive visitors at home, where the lighting is not always flattering.

We are speechless when our aged aunt, a widow, shows us a new studio portrait that has removed her double chins and every wrinkle—can't she see how ridiculous this is? We forget how politely she once looked at the snapshots we value most, wherein odd angles and certain laws of optics have combined to make our nose smaller and our legs much longer than they ever were in truth. Photographs lie, critics like to say. They don't lie enough, thinks our aunt, returning her framed picture to the family group on the mantel. If one considers the idealized photograph as a projected image of an ideal and resilient self, then we can use all the help we can get, stopping short of the lab table, thank you. A tasteful prop would be better, a piece of custom-built furniture which can be transported anywhere, along with a detailed instruction sheet: "How to Light Us Attractively."

A more or less healthy ego instructs us to groom ourselves, maintain or improve our looks, but an immature or perennially deficient ego begs, "Make me look like someone else." "And I look good in it, maybe it's because I'm tall, I'm the American woman type," says Choli, the sole speaker in Chapter Four of Manuel Puig's *Betrayed by Rita Hayworth* (1968). She is head of the local branch of Hollywood Cosmetics, so called because the agents of fashion and glamour in Argentina invariably bear French or American names. Choli looks like an ad for her company, "White-framed sunglasses with my [black] hair straightened and dyed auburn. . . . I brush [it] till it looks like silk, so dancing in a nightclub you can throw your head back and it's sexy falling down your shoulders." The time is 1941, the same year that George Hurrell photographed Ann Sheridan (b. Clara Lou Sheridan, right) and Eugene Richee helped Paramount Pictures transform an Ockleman into a Lake (preceding page).

Richee's portrait catches none of the charm Lake would display in her first major film, *Sullivan's Travels,* released that year, but it must have been a good fan magazine photo for a novice to study and follow in 1941 if she wanted a simple blueprint.

What Price Hollywood? (1932) had opened with a more challenging close-up, a tight shot of a crowded double-page magazine spread of ads and glamour pics which fills the entire screen. The camera pulls back to reveal a young woman (Constance Bennett) who proceeds to doll herself up according to the wide-ranging specifications on the page, from silk hose to the pucker-pout expression of the movie-love mouth. Such self-concern has its unattractive side, too, and Richee evokes it eerily if unintentionally in his photo of Veronica Lake. Her demure fingers, worthy of a cold-cream ad, touch her face all too tenderly; the hint of autoeroticism also alludes to furtive male activities. She might well be checking her pulse at the carotid artery, to be certain that her imitation of the submissive doll in the male supremacy fantasy has not gotten out of hand. Photos like Richee's tribute to terminal passivity told girls and young women to remember their place, unselfishly; Constance Ockleman's dream of perfection has not been fulfilled here. The light and focus are too harsh, too clear, her angle of repose all wrong, accentuating her overlip and the falseness of the lashes which deaden the eyes. Her hairline has been retouched crudely, and the left shoulder is too high, making her look lopsided, deformed, afflicted at least by a wryneck. She is not, as they say, very together. Could she be trying to straighten her head? Or has she been posed to death? Maybe the hands belong to someone else, the craftsman at the Hollywood Wax Museum who recently prepared The Bride of Frankenstein. Or she's really a fan magazine photomontage made from bits and pieces of different people, a symbol of—the fabricated or fragmented self? Or one may prefer to return to the lower road, as coursed by Cabrera Infante in his movie-impacted and verbally playful novel *Three Trapped Tigers* (1965), whose Havana revelers salute Cuba Venegas, "the most beautiful singer human eyes have heard, her hair styled

George Hurrell, *Ann Sheridan,* 1941.

a little like a mulatto version of Veronica Lake."

Richee's version of a poorly assembled or unfinished Miss Ockleman points toward one's basement or attic, or wherever old high school yearbooks are stored. Note how the girls are smiling in their sepia-tinted graduation photos, row upon row of little windows to the future, bravely smiling, it seems now, given the limitations of their cosmetic impersonations of popular movie stars, each yearbook a mirror of prevailing standards of beauty, and, possibly, "lifestyles," too: Class of 1944, Veronica Lake and Betty Grable; 1950, Jane Russell; 1955, Marilyn Monroe; 1960, Kim Novak; 1968, Faye Dunaway and Janis Joplin (the cinema's influence is fading fast); and, 1978, Farrah Fawcett and Mick Jagger. Watch teenagers as they stand before mirrors and scramble their neat, inert hair, thereby producing a wild and natural "contemporary look."

Motion picture actors used to be better-looking than everyone else, yet the props in old glamour photographs often seem to cast stars of the second magnitude as Everyman, ordinary people supported by elaborate crutches. If the sitter's presence or beauty failed to fill the blank space of the studio, the photographer had to do more than readjust the lights. If you were Ann Sheridan rather than Garbo, you got a form-fitting chaise longue and a photographer like George Hurrell, who would adjust your hand and arm until they were just so. What does an ordinary photographic subject do when he finds himself out in the open, at home, where most "portraits" are now taken by friendly if uninspired snapshooters? Instinctively, one moves away from a blank wall lest it make us look plain and boring. The new sofa would be okay, with the framed landscape above it, but it'd be better to go with something that stands for the "real you," maybe the bowling or skeet-shooting trophies grouped on top of the TV console. You can place one hand nonchalantly on the TV or even hold the latest trophy, thereby solving a big problem: what do you do with your hands when you pose? How do you hide your nervousness in life?

Major performers know exactly what to do with their hands. With or without the help of a photographer, actresses of the nineteen-thirties often choreographed digital arabesques which are far less arty than their possible source, Steiglitz's highly esteemed glamour pictures of his wife, Georgia O'Keeffe, whose photographed fingers sometimes constitute an entire Martha Graham dance sequence. Often enough, however, second-string stars didn't know what to do with their hands, either, a problem that is particularly glaring in the mid nineteen-forties, by which time twenty years worth of poses had exhausted the art—or is it craft?—of glamour photography. Betty Hutton thus brandishes a pair of pistols that fire little American flags (1944) and Glenn Ford stands primly in an over-decorated "oriental" living room (1946), one hand in his pocket, the other resting on the terracotta skull of a Buddha-like figurine that is laughing. (For these and other delirious absurdities, including Cary Grant playing a harp, see John Kobal's *Hollywood Color Portraits,* 1981.) Garbo is the only star of the thirties and forties who never used a prop, though sometimes even she donned a period costume from her latest film or enlisted the support of her graceful hands. The apparent self-confidence of the nameless young woman on the right seems almost heroic in this context. It is drawn from *Disfarmer* (1976), a collection of studio portraits taken by Mike Disfarmer in the tiny Ozark town of Heber Springs, Arkansas, during World War II. Using only a black or white backdrop and the natural light that came through a skylight, Disfarmer photographed his townspeople in an uncompromisingly direct way. They all stand and sit in a solemn, dignified manner, except for this woman, who must have struck this pose on her own, one imagines, in order to compete

Mike Disfarmer, Unidentified subject, ca. 1942.

with the pin-up pics on the barracks wall of her sweetheart, who is away in the service. She should have fared well. Her pose mimes Ann Sheridan, yet she's independent enough not to have raised her top lipline to the current forties level. Her upper hand signals the relaxed sexual authority of a star, but her full appeal is communicated by the tensely gripped thumb of her lower hand. This unidentified woman is not a brazen show-off, after all. She's the Unknown Soldier of portrait sitters, and, like Ann Sheridan at the end of her war film, she ought to receive a medal—unless it should go to Sheridan once more, for having managed to keep a straight face for the glamour camera in 1942 while seated amidst several large cakes of ice (see Kobal). Why aren't they melting?

To millions of young girls the world over, the ultimate pinnacle of achievement is to be a movie star," or so *Life* magazine asserted in its issue of January 29, 1940, in a picture-story headed "STARLETS ARE WORLD'S/MOST ENVIED OF GIRLS"—THANKS TO US, the headline writer might have added, for the sake of accuracy and cultural history. Although not as crass as the movie magazines, *Life* made it clear early on that "the full flavor of stardom, with its fabulous rewards of fame and wealth," was as compelling a subject as motion pictures per se. Imitators such as *Look, See, Click,* and *Pic* followed suit. During *Life*'s first run, 1936–72, only the Newsfronts section received more space than the Movie Department. One out of six covers of *Life* was given to a star or starlet; the "Movie of the Week" picture-story was always a tribute rather than a review. *Life*'s journalists propagated the myths of Hollywood as faithfully as did the hacks of the fanzines and the publicists for the studios, who, especially before the nineteen-fifties, found in *Life* a ready outlet for even the silliest examples of their glamour propaganda. Good specimens of the genre are offered in the popular assemblage *LIFE Goes to the Movies* (1975), particularly in the section titled "The Buildup." Embarrassed, perhaps, by what they found in the back files of *Life,* the book's loyal company editors claim that most of these "Buildup" photos were published originally in a "mock-serious" or "tongue-in-cheek" manner. This was not often the case, though the photograph on the right, by Loomis Dean, is drawn from an exceptionally amusing and mordant five-page spread about 20th

Century-Fox's attempts to make a star out of Colleen Townsend (August 30, 1948). Here she is shown being interviewed and arranged by the gossip columnist Hedda Hopper, who wants the starlet to conform with the rest of the bric-a-brac in Hedda's house. "DARLING, YOU'RE GOING PLACES!" reads the boldface caption in the 1948 version, where the words served as *Life*'s equivalent of a fatuous cinematic voice-over. Yet the "deadpan humor" claimed for "The Buildup" section is mainly a product of the self-conscious procedures of 1975; the new contexts, layouts, and captions provide a fascinating laboratory example of the sleight-of-hand nature of photojournalism, where a few words can so easily slant a picture.

Like a family album of old snapshots recently retouched and rearranged, *LIFE Goes to the Movies* gives little sense of the saccharine tone that pervades most of those starlet picture-spreads of the thirties and forties: brilliant sunshine, white flannels flapping in the warm Pacific breeze, indigo sky, full moon above the tropical trees—reason enough to smile in every photograph. The scandal-mongering in current celebrity magazines should not be confused with this perfect world, where even a merciless headhunter like Hedda Hopper is always treated with respect, notwithstanding her patent artificiality (note the glow of the photographer's strobe in the upper left of the picture).

To take one's place in this preternatural sun was to triumph as a pop version of the Young Man from the Provinces, as Lionel Trilling termed this figure from literature and history, who, in terms of the ar-

Loomis Dean, *Colleen Townsend and Hedda Hopper,* 1948. © 1948 Time, Inc.

chetype, could also be a woman (Amelia Earhart, Eva Perón). Motivated by pride and poverty, equipped only with intelligence, talent, and a sense of destiny, the Young Man from the Provinces transcended his mean and obscure origins by entering and conquering the important places, as in *The Great Gatsby* (b. Jay Gatz), or JEAN HARLOW—from EXTRA TO STAR (*Modern Screen,* August 1937), or THE RAPID/ RISE OF RUTH ROMAN, subtitled, "A single-minded dead-end kid from Boston makes her bid for a place as a big dramatic star in Hollywood" (*Life,*

May 1, 1950). The hopeful tyros in *Life*'s starlet story of 1940 are from Wallace, Idaho; Roosevelt, Utah; Coldwater, Mississippi; Venus, Texas. "Mary Healy in play suit was once a New Orleans typist," reads one of the captions in the story. "Lovely voice and figure now rate her high among starlets." Optimistic America, anyone might succeed!— except Colleen Townsend. After four film credits she retired in 1950 and rejoined her audience, with its scrapbooks and latest magazines, its memories and daydreams.

Movies and TV cast their spells, but motionless pictures in newspapers and magazines are arguably our primary study guides and touchstones, telling most of us what reality looks like and allowing us to measure our perceptions against such knowledge. In its heyday, *Life* magazine often asserted the authority of photographs by showing how new movies had in one way or another modeled scenes and performers on photos first published in their pages. "These [pictures] by LIFE Prove Facts in 'Grapes of Wrath'" declared the subhead in a picture-story of February 19, 1940, which re-published several of the FSA-like photos which the magazine had used earlier to document the truthfulness of Steinbeck's novel. The pictures were now paired with stills from the movie, *Life*'s usual mirror-image format for such evidence. Nor was it uncommon for their readers to be disappointed in a new film because it had looked better on the page as the "Movie of the Week." In order to compete with *Life* and the camera, commercial illustrators were forced to refine further their own illusionistic procedures and techniques, an artistically vulgar endeavor which produced the pin-ups of Varga and Petty as well as the more significant oeuvre of illustrators like Norman Rockwell.

Just as the subject of Rockwell's *Girl at the Mirror* (right) aspires to the mature beauty of the star in the photo, Jane Russell, so too did his paintings usually aspire to photography or the photographic. Starting in the late nineteen-thirties, Rockwell based his work on photos, sometimes using as many as 75 in the process of painting a single canvas. The success of his method is quite demonstrable. During World War II, for instance, his vision of the average G.I., Willie Gillis, appeared on eleven covers of *The Saturday Evening Post*. One cover (September 16, 1944) depicted a parlor wall bearing portraits of six generations of Gillises in the service, from the American Revolution through Willie, the bookshelf beneath them containing a row of amusing imaginary titles (*Great Loves of the Gillises, Gillis and Lincoln,* etc.). "After this appeared," Rockwell reported in 1946, "I received many letters from Gillises asking where they could purchase the books." *Girl at the Mirror* suggests that such dubious tributes must have bemused and sometimes disturbed the artist if not the illustrator. Like one of his most famous and most photographic works, *Freedom from Want* (the Thanksgiving dinner, 1943), *Girl at the Mirror* is cropped on the left as though it were a family snapshot—a worn old snap, in fact. Its cracked surface and ragged edges could be illusionistic touches. They are real, of course, evidence that this particular copy of the *Post,* recently hauled up from the basement, was once truly a family's magazine.

On a second look, however, the cover turns out to be one of Rockwell's least photographic of pictures. Although it was published in 1954, when Rockwell's skill was most proficient, *Girl* nevertheless seems unfinished, like the face of a woman interrupted at her cosmetic tray. The highly visible brushstrokes of the (brown) underpainting deliberately form a pattern or grisaille on the surface of the canvas, extending the assertive signature of an artist who here resists and

Norman Rockwell, *Girl at the Mirror,* 1954.

Photographer unknown, *Ladies' Lounge, Hollywood Theater, Sioux Falls, South Dakota,* 1937.

rejects the "next" stage in his procedure, the photographic perfectionism represented within the painting by a glamour photo, for the moment our touchstone of contrived and demoralizing "truthfulness." If the 1937 ladies' lounge of the Hollywood Theater, Sioux Falls, South Dakota (above) were empowered by Lewis Carroll to look into its own mirror and compare itself with Evelyn Hofer's 1977 photo of the second-mezzanine powder room designed by Donald Deskey at Radio City Music Hall (right), it too would find itself woefully lacking in style and glamour. But a young female member of the Sioux Falls audience, under the sway of movies and magazines, might take the provincial lounge for the M-G-M powder room on the *Tarzan* lot. Seeing her face encircled in the looking-glass, the girl would know for a few seconds what it feels like to be a starlet.

Evelyn Hofer, *Powder Room, Radio City Music Hall*, 1977.

Cosmetics commonly denote superficial self-improvement, but the fullest conceptions of the art or craft of makeup ask an audience to consider and imagine aspects of the self best kept at bay or ignored altogether. This routine publicity "two-shot" (right) of Warner Oland and Margarita Cansino in *Charlie Chan in Egypt* (1935), worthless until now, points toward the least complicated sort of fun manifest in bravura acting turns that are dependent upon makeup. Moviegoers once took special pleasure in impersonations such as Oland's Chan (seventeen films) and Akim Tamiroff's Chinese warlord in *The General Died at Dawn* (1936). One could measure the success of Oland's veritable disguise against the face of his son, always played by an actual oriental whose perfect U.C.L.A. English ("Okay, Pop!") served as a comic foil for his father's wise maxims in stereotypical pidgin English. Sympathetic to the idea and implications of impersonation and disguise, audiences were eager to be in on the act, at least vicariously. Magazines of the thirties and forties obliged them, granting almost as much space to elaborate makeup procedures as they did to backstage views of large-scale studio artifice (the vast Chinese farm and village built by M-G-M for *The Good Earth,* the typhoon machines it used on *The Hurricane,* both 1937).

Picture-stories about ambitious makeup schemes stressed the number of hairs it took to make a wolf man, the amount of time necessary to apply the stuff (six hours for Lon Chaney, Jr., in 1941), the exact weight of false appendages and padding, the literally painful circumstances of transformation, man into monster and back again. Horror movies were deemed too lowbrow to receive much coverage, which is amusing now, given the continued life of such movies and the graveyard status of the "prestige" biographies valued so highly. *Life* magazine's reverential treatment of film bios such as *The Life of Emile Zola* (1937) and *The Remarkable Andrew* (1942) formulated a middle-class insistence on the public values of supposedly educational materials, the superego putting the lid on the "trash"-inclined id. The "Motion Pictures" section in the old *Encyclopaedia Britannica* (1962 edition) complements the magazine's emphasis by devoting three pages of photographs to the "Art of Makeup," one series of shots of actors in those particular film bios revealing how Montagu Love and Paul Muni were made into George Washington and Emile Zola, aging considerably in the process.

Readers were fascinated by the spectacle of aging. *Life* showed how Sam Jaffee gained two hundred years in *Lost Horizon* (1937); *Photoplay* documented the deline of thirty-six-year-old Charles Laughton as Rembrandt, a most affecting performance. "Isn't this a wonderful makeup job? It's Charles Laughton aging dramatically for 'Rembrandt' " (the heading above three stills in *Photoplay,* September 1935). It *is* wonderful, partly because we're in on the illusionistic game, the trick, and, like a character actor who each night leaves his cosmetic burden in the dressing room, we can go home from the theater, renewed by the performance, unscathed for now by the "makeup" in question. But Oland's charade might not be admired now by Chinese-American viewers of the Late

Photographer unknown, Warner Oland and Margarita Cansino in *Charlie Chan in Egypt,* 1935.

Show, and the awkwardness of Margarita Cansino's "Egyptian girl" is telescoped here by her positively Balinese hand gestures, her jejune miming of "fear," all of which may be appropriate; as Confucius say, "Life is B-picture, not perfect M-G-M show." But Cansino improved. The studio raised her hairline, bleached her, retouched her, changed her name to— turn page for correct answer.

The essential makeup (i.e., composition) of an evolving self is best delineated by words, not pictures. A verbal turn or two on the page, however, can make this evocative but hopelessly inarticulate portrait of Tyrone Power (right) mirror the most private reaches of Puig's novel, *Betrayed by Rita Hayworth.* "A monkey!" exclaimed Darryl F. Zanuck in 1935 when he viewed the first screen test of bushy-browed Tyrone Power. A year later Power was starring in *Lloyd's of London* (right), thanks to the eyebrow tweezers of Hollywood Cosmetics, to use the generic name coined by Puig for *Betrayed by Rita Hayworth,* whose movie theater provides a kind of plasma for the residents of its isolated Argentine town from 1933 to 1948, the duration of the novel (see p. 96). Its principal focus is the developing consciousness of young Toto Casals, who is bright and sensitive, movie-mad, and much pampered by several women. His passion as a child is to draw movie picture-cards with his mother and color in glamour photos of actresses. They are his icons, and, in a book awash with the names of films and performers, Toto's preferences partake of a coherent iconography that at once reflects and rejects the ethics of the Church and the state of Latin machismo. "In [the] communion book there was a saint just like Norma Shearer, a nun with a white costume and some white flowers in her hand," Toto muses in one of his interior monologues early in the novel, when he is six. "I have pictures of her serious, laughing, and in profile cut out of every magazine. . . ." "I'm going to be good, like Shirley [Temple]," thinks Toto, whose favorite stars—Shearer,

Ginger Rogers, Luise Rainer in *The Great Ziegfeld* (1936)—are vulnerable, friendly, sexually unthreatening, "good girls" all. Actors are a negligible presence to Toto; an Astaire-Rogers film is called "the one of Ginger Rogers and the guy who dies." When Toto is nine, his favorite film is *Blood and Sand* (1941), in which Rita Hayworth humiliates matador Tyrone Power, "him kneeling like an idiot." Toto tries to admire Rita despite her wickedness, because his troubled and distant father—a Hayworth enthusiast—has for once accompanied his wife and son to the cinema, an occasion cherished by the boy. "But [Rita] betrays the good boy," thinks Toto, who must reject her. He must, before she—her kind—can hurt him, and for once Toto quietly but tellingly identifies with an actor (thus the novel's title). *Spellbound,* Hitchcock's blatantly "Freudian" mystery thriller of 1945, is Toto's favorite movie when he is thirteen, and *Betrayed by Rita Hayworth* turns out to be a most teasing Freudian mystery—clues aplenty as to Toto's emerging sexual self, especially his deeply feminine identification and his "classic" Oedipal bind—but no answer to the rude question, Will Toto Turn Out to Be Homosexual? "Only [the] saints can see . . . Toto hiding to color in the faces and dresses of the actresses," his female cousin observes when Toto, age nine, is forbidden such activities. The end of the novel finds the fifteen-year-old boy in hiding, so to speak, like everyone else in *Betrayed,* especially the men, who have been silenced by machismo and sentenced to the solitary confinement of their interior monologues (see p. 77), a place where metaphoric

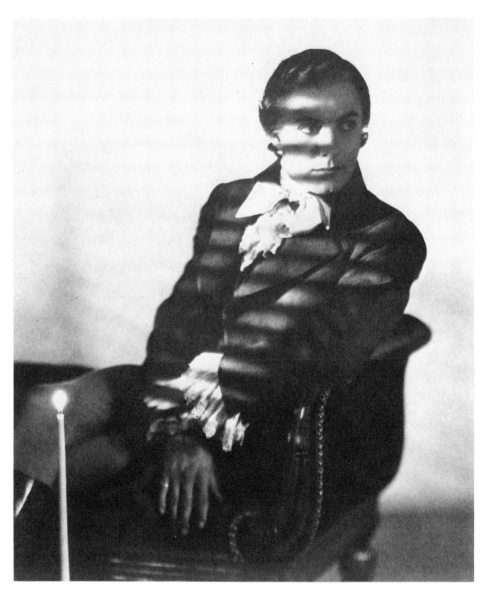

Photographer unknown, Tyrone Power in *Lloyds of London, 1936.*

prison-bar shadows ought to fall, as in this photo of Tyrone Power. About to emerge from obscurity, the young actor had been warned by his studio to hide his homosexuality—in the shadows, it would seem, where viewers would be less likely to notice that the "good boy," Tyrone Power, seems to be metamorphosing through a lap-dissolve into Margarita Cansino (p. 107), who would soon become Rita Hayworth. In time, she too was betrayed by "Rita Hayworth."

Ernest Bachrach, *Dolores Del Rio,* 1931.

Glamour photography has come out of hiding in recent years, as quietly and gracefully as the way each successive handsome brunette head has blended with the next one here, culminating in Greta Garbo (overleaf, right). Ernest Bachrach took this publicity picture (above) of Dolores Del Rio (b. Lolita Dolores Asunsolo de Martinez) in 1931, for RKO, and John Kobal made it respectable in 1980, when he included it in his book *The Art of the Great Hollywood Portrait Photographers.* Many collections of such pictures were published during the nineteen-seventies, but this was the first one that dared to declare its contents "art." What *is* art? Or beauty? "Beauty is truth, truth beauty" may still serve veteran collectors of Greek vases, but the new adepts of glamour photography must yearn for a more up-to-date and concrete vocabulary. Kobal's 1980 collection was well received, for at least three reasons: he had chosen excellent images, which, no longer compromised by their original fan magazine context, were given an additional lift by photography's ever-rising prestige. Excavations are under way everywhere. Baron Adolf de Meyer's lustrous soft-focus studio close-ups of flowers and glassware, removed from their original context as ads or fashion layouts in *Vogue* and *Vanity Fair* between 1914 and 1921, are now seen as small masterworks of the Pictorialist school, reminiscent of the early art photographs of Steichen. Whatever its present context, however, the Del Rio photo is on its own as a photograph. Unlike Garbo, say (b. Greta Gustafson), or Joan Crawford (b. Lucille le Sueur), Del Rio and her old films signify nothing to most contemporary viewers. She never had a strong screen identity or persona, not even in her prime. Unable to draw on or summon a prop that would telescope her appeal (Steichen's chrysanthemums for Anna May Wong), Bachrach instead turned her into the principal design component of an arrangement as harmonious as the second mezzanine ladies' powder room at Radio City Music Hall, where the severe outlines and geometric motifs of Donald Deskey's 1931 Art Deco furnishings are softened and complemented by the mellow colors and fleshy Art Nouveau curves of

Yasuo Kuniyoshi's mural (p. 105), a floral fantasia whose monumental yellow tulips (left side) are equal to the scale of the Music Hall and perhaps Paradise, too. If Bachrach had convinced Del Rio to pose with her arms at her side or behind her back (there is no evidence that he tried, but it improves the story to say that he did), then the composition would have been even more stylized in the manner of the streamlined black-and-white Hollywood sets of the time, with their matching performers (such as Astaire and Rogers in their RKO pictures). But Del Rio refused to be posed to death. Her hands seem instead to embrace life, almost literally, as though she were holding a small child. The lower hand is particularly maternal, and it warms the entire picture. The upper hand is ambiguously expressive, being at once self-protective, demure, and seductive at the juncture where that one elegant finger disappears into the black silk, calling attention to her wedding ring, a unique stroke and fissure in the field of artifice, signaling that this is a person rather than a prop or objet d'art. "Del Rio," simply enough, was the name of her first husband. Her puffed sleeves and high neckline signal decorum, as opposed to the open sexuality of Ann Sheridan and Disfarmer's anonymous subject (pp. 97 and 99). In terms of pure design, the arms and hands of Bachrach's subject represent Art Nouveau refusing to become Art Deco, a colder style. If assimilation of beauty is your only wish, then Dolores Del Rio is a masterpiece of Gallé glass, perfectly displayed and lighted to please your eye.

Since her retirement from films at the age of thirty-five (1941), Greta Garbo has been in hiding, especially from cameras, thus sustaining the illusion created on the silver screen that her beauty is impervious to time. The enduring appeal of Edward Steichen's 1928 portrait of her (right), perhaps the signal masterpiece of glamour photography, is based on the extent to which he at once predicts and captures her myth, her enviable condition. Although Steichen photographed her at the M-G-M studio for the pages of *Vanity Fair,* he here avoids any heavy-duty props, but not artifice, since the pose helps to transform Garbo into something of a symbol. This is how each of us deserves to be photographed: flattering yet tasteful lighting, no concessions to convention, our good looks recorded but our dignity and privacy left intact, a nice way to be remembered. Garbo's eyes are wide open, unlike those of Ann Sheridan's or Veronica Lake's. She posed as she pleased, as Steichen and others have said. Her gaze is steady—"Today's Woman," some might say, "no one's Gallé dish." Yet her pose also calls to mind the Sphinx, investing her with the aura of agelessness (enhanced in the original print by sepia tonalities). By wearing basic black and covering her hair, Garbo seems to be protecting herself against the winds of change, the whims of fads and fashions. Only her plucked eyebrows are dated, but they don't look silly now, like Ann Sheridan's slithery gown, come-hither posture, and droopy eyelids, doomed conventions of "sexiness" moored in their period. Of course Ann and movie fans were no more amused by that photo in 1941 than we first were by those pictures of ourselves and our friends and families which today make us smile and sometimes laugh out loud. Here's a photo of us at the senior prom, a pompadoured scarecrow in a cavernous white dinner jacket, the sleeves extending to our knuckles, the bowtie askew, and we remember how good we looked in the bathroom mirror, how handsome we felt all night. Here's one we should burn or bury, taken ten years later, an expensive studio portrait of the boy as a young professional: the "serious" expression is all wrong, the "determined" brow is furrowed much too self-consciously—Karsh would have stuck a globe of the world in the foreground. We laugh now in order to reassure ourselves that recent snapshots and portraits will not look foolish one day, that the "look" or "personality" structured by transient fashions in cosmetics and clothes and poses will for once turn out to be as durable and consistent as less photogenic properties such as our attitudes and ideas, our character and identity. Or we laugh because our makeup is not altogether right, in place, and we know it, unlike our aging sisters who believe they have preserved their prime by retaining the hairdos and liplines of 1942, as though they were life-size high school graduation pictures of themselves, on their feet and breathing. "Ida Lupino," coiffed as she was in *High Sierra,* sells us a ticket at the theater. After the show, "Maureen O'Hara" in eyeglasses waits on your table, her head topped by a high rust-colored beehive. "It's a wig," sniggers a girl at a nearby table. "Ann Sheridan," the nurse, bends

Edward Steichen, *Greta Garbo,* 1928.

over me and checks my oxygen again, and I'm glad to see her, and maybe her dated makeup, too, enhanced now by a soft, indirect light from the hallway. Otherwise, it's dark in the room. What time is it? Three a.m., she says, giving me a painless injection in one of my I.V. tubes. Did she really look like Ann Sheridan, or had I given myself at least thirty-four more years to live by placing myself back in the early nineteen-forties, in the hands of the past?

THE PAINFUL TRUTH

Clarence Sinclair Bull, *Buster Keaton,* 1932.

"Make my picture look natural—I don't want you to flatter me," says the woman in a Rube Goldberg cartoon of 1911, from his open-ended series "Phoney Films." Seated in front of a dropcloth for her formal photo, she is cross-eyed, has only one tooth, arms like an orangutan, and hair wound so tightly in a bun that it looks like a doorknob. Given the ethic and habits of phoney filmers everywhere, from Main Street to Hollywood, she probably didn't get her wish, though the situation isn't hopeless; we are quite able to absorb the worst news about ourselves implicit in photographs of others.

Buster Keaton may not be cross-eyed in this M-G-M publicity portrait (left) by Clarence Sinclair Bull, 1932, but he does "look natural," for the pose, decor, dress, and lighting combine to suggest human depths uncharacteristic of the glamour genre or of M-G-M, then the grand coordinator and orchestrator of sentimental styles and bourgeois values (1925–50). An unhatted Buster is Keaton unmasked, made fragile, and *mask* is the key word. The stoical deadpan of the great silent clown has given way to the face of an apprehensive man whose actual circumstances would soon realize the worst expectations of his cinematic projection. At odds with M-G-M and talking pictures, Keaton was at the edge, drinking heavily and self-destructively, about to begin his long and terrible slide, and C. S. Bull records that here. Every detail works. The striped pants and Art Deco belt proffer a Keaton who is à la mode, a sport, but the closed button on his shirt signals tension. The rope and pilings allude to Keaton's triumphant past, hits such as *The Navigator* (1924) and *Steamboat Bill, Jr.* (1928), in which Buster is spared when a cyclone collapses a frame building upon him. But nothing will save him in this picture, the cutting edge of the threatening plank catching Clarence Bull's prescient Expressionist light as well as the brunt of hindsight. Keaton is on the scaffold, a stationary target, a rare posture for the vulnerable but acrobatic Buster. He made only one more feature-length picture, which was released the following year. Props tell the truth, for a change. The other photographs in this section of the book also present diminished spaces and various "doublings" which express the sort of truths eschewed by "Phoney Films," especially those of M-G-M, where darkness was not a favored mood or tonality.

At first glance it might appear that Lee Friedlander's *New York City, 1963* (right) is the product of a sudden nostalgia awakened by his surprising discovery of a miraculously preserved Mickey Rooney: Mickey before his eight marriages, Mickey the No. 1 male box-office attraction of 1940, the Andy Hardy of Saturday matinees, his framed portrait at Woolworth's—remember how the aging floorboards sagged underfoot at Woolworth's?—Mickey young and beaming in the main windows of our youth (Friedlander and this viewer were born the same year). But anyone familiar with Friedlander's work of the early sixties will recognize that this picture is characteristic of him, and also of his two great masters, Eugène Atget (1857–1927) and Walker Evans (1903–75). By their example, they instructed subsequent street photographers and documentarians to turn their backs on the main action and shoot the form and substance of unlikely spaces (see the photograph on p. 41, by Shahn, Evans's first pupil and 1932 roommate). Evans's best-known pictures of pictures appear in his classic collection, *American Photographs* (1938). It has taught countless Americans how to regard their indigenous environment, and the titles of several important books acknowledge the Evans enterprise and sway: *American Interiors* (1978), by Chauncey Hare; *The American Monument* (1976), by Friedlander, which has as its point of departure two war memorials in the work of Evans; and *The Americans* (1959), by Robert Frank, whose debt to Evans has recently been exaggerated.

Mickey Rooney's presence makes this an eminently American window, though adepts of the photography avant-garde would sneer if Mickey were deemed the only subject here. By choosing to "document" (one now uses the verb advisedly) a dreary commercial window, where he discovers aesthetically marvelous forms and intriguing visual conundrums, Friedlander pulls the proverbial rug out from under the conventional spectator. Is that ghostly Chevrolet a reflection or the thing itself, moored on the side street? Does the shard of a car in the lower left of the photograph mirror movement from behind the camera? Is the overlapping lighter-toned area a celluloid curtain on the front pane, Friedlander's chimerical picture plane? And could the large empty frame behind Rooney be a mirror? Its abstract patterns and shadows may defy analysis as to the light source, but, along with the fragments and strips of cardboard, they certainly do define an unexpected kind of order and progression, from *objets trouvés* to collage—modern art, of all things!—Picasso or Braque from about 1914, the empty frame alone a canvas by Franz Kline. Compositionally right, and amazingly so, the larger frame is also ambiguous and darkly ominous, a curiously tense form ready to—to what? If it suggests negative space, then its white-jacketed and trusting neighbor clearly resides in a space that is positive in every way, as distanced from the drab and crowded circumstances of this urban environment as Andy Hardy was from any quotidian. Solemnly said, to be sure, but the willful optimism of Mickey's guardian, old M-G-M, is too manifestly American to forget. Its glossy escapism could trav-

Lee Friedlander, *New York City, 1963.*

esty authentic emotions, hurtfully, perhaps, as in their version of Saroyan's *The Human Comedy* (1943), set in a prelapsarian small town during World War II, with Mickey Rooney featured as Ulysses the Western Union boy. At the end of the movie his older brother, Pvt. Van Johnson, is killed overseas. Mickey goes to deliver the message to his mom but destroys it when he sees that his brother's best Army buddy, a wounded orphan with a limp, has arrived at their doorstep. "Ma, the soldier's home!" announces Mickey, the

vagueness of his reference implying that she may not notice the substitution. Van's ghost follows them through the door as *The Human Comedy* concludes. The shallow space of Friedlander's window is Mickey's true element, the dark frame representing the depths from which M-G-M recoiled. The rose is still blooming in Mickey's lapel, but only in Friedlander's window and in the solarium of nostalgia, a crowded, steamy place these days, its floorboards sinking dangerously low beneath all the weight.

Joan Crawford remains the quintessential female star because she outdid all competitors in creating and sustaining over a span of four decades an illusion of agelessness and indestructibility, an especially American triumph because it was so clearly the product of constant hard work rather than the reward due an M-G-M goddess (such as Garbo). This became evident only in the years following her comeback at Warner Bros. in the nineteen-forties, *her* forties (*Mildred Pierce,* 1945). Indomitable in life as well as in popular art, Crawford was among that handful of female stars who, says Otto Preminger, "survived by acting like men." This aspect of her life and career accounts, obviously, for her popularity among female impersonators and camp followers of the nineteen-sixties, who adored even her silliest roles—or, perhaps, *especially* those roles, since they were so patently a matter of performance, of *style,* however high-pitched and florid.

Style—the word certainly suits this striking 1932 glamour portrait (right) that George Hurrell did of her for M-G-M. Nothing if not up-to-date, he realizes a classical impulse by way of Art Deco and the De Stijl movement in Europe, which emphasized geometrical rigor. Marble, columns, and an austerely draped figure are arranged in order to depict the star as a life-size icon or objet d'art, completing the job begun on Dolores Del Rio (p. 110). The sterling silver urn and the alabaster head (available, no doubt, at Tiffany's, as a set) partake of the same horizon line, and nature *is* on the line here. The womanly contours of the body are well-disguised, the hand

and wrist (bottom right) wrapped in a scarf so as to suggest that the bare arm could well be another column. Hurrell's little scarf stratagem emphasizes the importance of Del Rio's hands and arms arabesque and the way it holds off the camera. Note how Crawford's other hand is minimized by overexposure, the sleeve flush left, insisting on pattern and surface instead of life and depth. This space is more shallow, literally, than Mickey Rooney's window, and short on air, though this poses no hazard to a prop or zombie. Hurrell's Crawford suggests that the highest ideal of beauty and perfection is deathly, a very old story indeed, pointing ahead to Joan as the "Belle Dame sans Merci" of several melodramas. The photo is doubly eerie because it is Crawford, rather than the less forceful Del Rio, who has been stilled. She is nothing if not artifice. The seams show, if one looks twice, as at trompe l'oeil wall art. Notice the shabbiness of the column on the left and the worn edges of the window sash; the sectioned "marble" is probably the nineteen-thirties equivalent of contact paper. And isn't that a radiator behind her? Perhaps the urn is made of chrome rather than sterling silver. Hurrell has disguised and transformed a very prosaic space.

Crawford's face, covered with freckles in earlier publicity pictures, has now been treated by the same corporate light as Mickey Rooney's, the brilliant, even beam which also illuminates virtually every corner of *Meet Me in St. Louis* (1944), that representative yet excellent M-G-M production. Save for one nocturnal scene, shadows and death are banned from the set, a Technicolor version of 1903 as true to life as Craw-

George Hurrell, *Joan Crawford*, 1932.

ford's kitchen here. Concurrent with such war-time nostalgia is the rise of *film noir,* whose collective vision of loneliness, despair, and dread was necessary because it assured an audience that its own suppressed fears were shared human responses; *Meet Me in St. Louis, Bathing Beauty,* and *Pin-up Girl,* all from 1944, were balanced or counteracted by the same year's *Double Indemnity, The Woman in the Window,* and *Phantom Lady,* films in which death and night are one. Most of the photos in this section of the book are to the glamour genre what *film noir* is to the standard Metro-Goldwyn-Mayer fare.

Robert Frank's *photo noire* of 1956, titled *Detroit* (right), incisively describes a human predicament. The principal feature on the double bill is *A Woman's Face,* a recycled 1941 M-G-M melodrama. "Joan Crawford" proclaims the sign above the booth, but the woman in the ticket window, whose coiffure is also vintage 1941, doesn't measure up. Although the ironic counterpoint created by the ticket-seller's face and the star's glamour is clear enough, the appeal of the photograph is more subtle. (NOW SHOWING) it reads in parentheses, beneath the woman's face, and she surely is a parenthetical and insubstantial person, like a snapshot of herself—FOTOS 25¢ WHILE-U-WAIT—contained and circumscribed by the signs and all those movie stills; indeed, many who view this picture at first fail to discern her. The circular device on her window suggests the voice box in a prison visiting room, the breathing space for a crated creature. The naked light bulbs, reminiscent of a circus side show, shadow her face expressively, in the low-key manner of a forties *film noir*. Note, however, that every image of Joan is brightly illumined by the steady beam and grief-proof glow of high-key lighting.

The ticket-seller's face occupies an imperfect rectangular area analogous to the dimensions of the numerous stills, a spatial setup that transforms and reduces her to but one of many flat images in a montage arrangement, a component in a veritable trompe l'oeil. Lost in space, she is threatened too by the camera's dislocated angle of vision (Robert Frank's conscious intention? intuition? accident?), which has tipped her world to the right. Instability, if not entropy, has been visualized. The woman's mute and bemused sadness—or inner space—is counterpointed further by images of Joan Crawford warmed by companionship—a solicitous man (above left), a child (above the booth)—these tensions recalling the relationship, formal and otherwise, between the two picture frames in Lee Friedlander's window. But the ticket-seller's mental set may find its ultimate expression in Crawford's alarm and terror: the splash enlargement as alter ego, this picture's darkest frame, possibly. The entire photograph might well be titled *A Woman's Faces.* And if this were a totally managed and premeditated scene, the setup of a sardonic movie director or highly allusive and Pop-infused novelist (Nabokov, Pynchon, or Manuel Puig), one could be certain that the film title had been carefully chosen—a sign, rather than symbol, that reminds us of Crawford's role as a woman whose face is hideously disfigured on the right side. Morally crippled by her unhappy physiognomy, she falls among criminals, but is finally redeemed by love and last-minute plastic surgery. The high-key lighting has prevailed, as befits so consistent and pervasive a metaphor, the signature of sunny M-G-M. The splash enlargement, after all, is only one-dimensional, the alarm and terror contrived, unintentionally amusing: every hair is in place on that perfectible object (or surface), Joan Crawford's head. Literally and figuratively distanced from *that* Hollywood, this frank Detroit posits no happy ending.

Robert Frank, *Detroit,* 1956.

Because she was the most durable and frequently photographed female star, Crawford's face became ubiquitous and iconic, eventually making her the ideal object and springboard for all kinds of artists. Milton Caniff used her as the principal model for the Dragon Lady (b. 1937) in his *Terry and the Pirates*. James Rosenquist's *Untitled (Joan Crawford Says)*, 1964 (right), in its large format—92 by 78 inches—takes fuller measure of Joan, and, more deeply, of photography and the photographic. A mock-photo as well as a mock-monumental ad, *Untitled* slyly draws upon salient features of Joan and the glamour genre in order to diminish the star. This Joan is overlit, relentlessly, the lights denying her hair full body and turning her face into a veritable blank space keyed to the one-dimensional rectangle above her. Unblinking, she seems mesmerized by the beam, her stiff smile the product of Novocaine or held at half-mast to prevent wrinkles. Beauty *is* skin-deep. Millions of moviegoers may have considered Crawford their imago, and followed her advice, but who could care what this Joan Crawford says, despite the cursive intimacy and sincerity of those three words, in Joan's very own hand?

The "cropping" of any coherent commercial message makes Joan appear even more foolish, as when we turn off the sound on TV, locking a performer in the absurdity of dissociated expression and gesture—the effect, too, of that precursor of Pop Art, the splash enlargement of Crawford photographed by Robert Frank. The startling size of *Untitled* (in height, seven feet plus) is equivalent to the total surround of popular culture, imagined here as one huge yet insufficient space containing a collective sign or cliché from the "media," in this case the 1964 avatar of the star, culled from movie magazines and from *Life, Look,* et cetera; from cigarette ads and tours in behalf of Pepsi; from old movies on the tube and new ones in CinemaScope. The monumentality of *Untitled* is not altogether mock. Given its scale, the iconic image is as strange as it is familiar: one can never *see* such a Joan, not even in a theater, inasmuch as this "blow-up" seems to imitate a page from a magazine spread yet has been framed to indicate that it is a balanced composition by an artist. The dots of the photoengraver's screen should be discernible on so large a "page," as in Roy Lichtenstein's large comic book panels, but Rosenquist proffers an old-fashioned painterly system of closed brush strokes—a work in the museum tradition. He addresses here and elsewhere the issues that Norman Rockwell raised, or stumbled upon, a decade earlier in a single painting (p. 103).

What seemed so real in *Untitled* is wittily illusionistic and fantastic, pointing toward the bland and blind ways in which we trust that supposedly most truthful of forms, the unmediated photograph. To win that trust, advertising artists and commercial illustrators have for years based their work on photographs or photo projections, and *Untitled* at once reflects pictorial technology and comments upon it. In Chesterfield's magazine ads of the forties one can't be sure at first if the pretty "Girl of the Month" is a painting or a color photo (it was the former). The

James Rosenquist, *Untitled (Joan Crawford Says)*, 1964. Original painting in color.

crucial issue in *Untitled,* however, is rhetoric rather than verisimilitude. The ad agency representing Paramount Pictures wrote *Life* magazine in 1936, "We're going to run you ragged—copy your technique so that you can't tell ads from editorial pages." The success of such cosmetic disguises is attested to by the barely discernible clarification, ADVERTISEMENT, which often appears above an ad. Rosenquist posits the circumstances of an almost totally visual culture, when the world will turn on one word set in minuscule type, on a voice-over or caption or title more exact than *Untitled.*

The fullest measure of Crawford has been taken here (right) by an undistinguished and anonymous portrait painter who knows that photos often lie. Preserved by Nathan Lyons in an untitled photograph that was shot in Los Angeles, 1972, this pairing or doubling of frames and faces reverses the basic convention of the Before and After self-improvement diptych. A photo taken when she was well into her fifties, the smaller Crawford image shares the window with other ageless forces and well-preserved specimens; the nearby array of pressed flowers and decorative weeds, too good to be true, is a setup for the explicator, who secretly hopes that the glamour shot is from *Autumn Leaves* (1956), where Joan marries a man half her age. Crawford's eternal September was not entirely a wonder of nature, of course.

Eve Arnold's collection of photos, *The Unretouched Woman* (1976), includes a unit depicting Crawford's cosmetic regimen, her face variously covered with thick grease, gauze wrappings, and eye compresses, all in tight close-up—a grim report from the war zone by Larry Burrows or David Douglas Duncan. I had seen these and other Crawford photos early one morning in 1959, in their original context, a magazine feature timed to coincide with the release of her new movie, *The Best of Everything*. This spread also showed Joan enduring hours of grueling daily exercise and, in a penultimate shot, a half-dressed Joan standing proudly in her blouse and corset, a gladiator almost ready for combat. I went to see the film that afternoon, at an expensive Broadway movie theater. When Crawford first appeared on the CinemaScope screen—trim, handsome, heroic in scale—a harsh female voice directly behind us exulted, "She looks *terrible*!" I turned to view the critic, a fiftyish woman weighing around two hundred pounds, wearing an old cotton housedress, box lunch on her lap, curlers in her hair—A.W.O.L. from a Weegee photo or Russell Lee's Texas living room (p. 24). She and her companion, who nodded solemnly, would sympathize with the motive force behind the portrait of Crawford in the window. Even when she "aged" in a film, Crawford did so on her own terms. Witness *Mildred Pierce,* where one streak of silver was added to her hair, or Robert Aldrich's perversely funny *What Ever Happened to Baby Jane?* (1962), in which Joan—paralyzed and evil—is nevertheless allowed to expire on a beach, dressed in virginal white, her famous sculpted face taking the sun quite nicely, thank you. Our painter will have none of this. Using the glamour shot as a model, she restores the work of time (for some reason I perceive the artist as a woman), producing a sad and bitter Crawford, a Dorian Gray–like image which magically preshadows her daughter's book of bad news about the star's true character and behavior, *Mommie Dearest* (1978).

Although the portrait and the seascape to its left have been painted by different hands, they are paired in identical frames, aptly enough, inasmuch as the pictures depict the flow and ebb of inexorable forces. Crawford's white dress has been changed in the painting to a signal black. A far more subtle [un]refinement is the altered line of Joan's upper lip, now a more "common" or vulgar configuration. An

Nathan Lyons, Untitled, 1972.

American icon has been grounded, turned into an aging Fifth Avenue matron and given a white fox stole (draped impossibly) for her promenade but, cruel denial, no veil to disguise her suddenly visible signs of decline. In life, she would have wrapped the fox stole around her neck, the way Karsh of Ottawa took advantage of Hemingway's cowl-neck sweater to soften the unpleasant expression on the aging writer's face (1957). Give her a break! you want to tell the painter—drape that funny-looking white elephant's trunk around her neck and chin. But this artist rejects such artifice. It is as if that dark and empty larger frame in Lee Friedlander's New York window had contained a recent portrait of an aging Mickey, preferably by Avedon or Diane Arbus. Indeed, had Arbus been a painter, this "Joan Crawford" is probably what an Arbus oil portrait of the aging movie queen would have looked like.

Were Rube Goldberg's grotesque sitter here today she would have received her due from Avedon, Arbus, or any one of the young photographers in their wake whose unsparing images have contributed so much to a revived form of sentimental Expressionism. Its dictum seems to be "ugly is truth, truth ugly." (In movies, this equation takes form in the predictable grotesqueries of Robert Altman's *A Wedding* [1978] in place of the predictable sunshine of M-G-M's *Father of the Bride* [1950], and in photography, the consistently Grosz-like wedding covered by Larry Fink in *American Images* [Renato Danese, ed., 1979] as opposed to the formulaic commercial nuptial photography gathered by Barbara Norfleet in *Wedding* [1979].)

The idealized photos offered by the glamour galleries and neighborhood studios of yore often realized vain dreams, of course, but what truths do the most candid of Arbus's calculated pictures suggest or document? *Woman with a Veil on Fifth Avenue, New York City, 1968* is one of Arbus's more genial and relaxed subjects, though the photographer probably hasn't flattered her here (right). Indeed, this kind of shot may confirm the fears of that first-nighter who recoiled from Weegee in Simon Nathan's photo (p. 36). Yet the charges of an untoward aggressiveness sometimes lodged against Arbus are complicated by the fact that most of her photos are collaborative. Unlike, say, the victims of Weegee's infrared treatment in the dark theater (p. 74), Arbus's very willing subjects are aware of the camera, and it is self-awareness, in the largest sense, that makes

such pictures so compelling. The veiled woman smiles with the confidence of a Joan Crawford. *Good for her!* we exclaim; evidently she doesn't think she is . . . well, let's call her ordinary-looking. Of course, she may have been disarmed by Arbus, a "reformed" fashion photographer who could still coax a pose out of her subjects, or make them feel that they were being stopped by a familiar, trustworthy street personality like Jimmy Jemail, for fifty years the ubiquitous "Inquiring Fotographer" of the New York *Daily News*. (Arbus was the shaping spirit behind the Museum of Modern Art's 1973 show, *From the Picture Press*, whose raw tabloid images were possibly as liberating to her as primitive art had been to Expressionists such as Emil Nolde.) One may presume, moreover, that this woman's cultural expectations are positive. Like our children, she has known nothing but kindness, in this case from "friendly" middle-class cameras: posed "candids" made at weddings and on holiday—mostly harmless medium or long shots—and those glowing re-creations from the nearest health spa, the local portrait studio. If she were at all knowledgeable about photography, however, she wouldn't smile about the prospects of being shot point blank at high noon by a waist-high camera supported by a flashgun. The resulting picture has penetrated her cosmetic defenses, melted her mask; the area around the eyes is particularly hard hit, and so is the chin (or chins). Perhaps she *has* been taken, but so have we, in the stricter visual sense of the verb, and herein lies the strength of the photo. Already in dramatic (or ironic) close-up, the woman is

Diane Arbus, *Woman with a Veil on Fifth Avenue, New York City, 1968.*

thrust further toward us by the blurred focus of the city behind her, squeezed so close to the picture plane that her breath threatens to fog the glass. We're face to face with a smiling stranger, an uncomfortable situation. Do I know her? Wish she'd stop smiling. She's too close, she's violating my space—and, for once, contemporary jargon *connects.* The intimacy is unsettling because we're in *her* space, too; her vulnerability is ours, the capacity for doubling apparent in Bull, Friedlander, Frank, and Lyons having now

extended out of the photo to include the viewer. If seeing is knowing, then self-knowledge is a rare and precious achievement. Be fitted for a new dress or suit and discover a stranger in the three-way mirror. Look at your expression in that snapshot taken without your knowledge at a party and learn what the definitive sad sack looks like. Stare dumbly at your X-ray and wait for the doctor to diagnose it. Confront Diane Arbus's touchingly confident matron as you would consider an uncompromising mirror.

The celebrity portraits that Edward Steichen produced in the twenties and thirties for *Vanity Fair* and *Vogue* are widely admired as the finest of their period. Beaumont Newhall's *The History of Photography* (1964) states, "They form a pictorial biography" of their subjects, "succeed[ing] best with people of the [cinema and] theatre"—which, in a word, is wrong. Along with his Garbo (p. 113), Steichen's *Gloria Swanson, New York, 1924* (right) is often singled out as a masterpiece of photographic portraiture. It is a beautiful image in the way that Art Nouveau can be beautiful, but it's really a kind of anti-portrait. (It was originally printed in a lovely umber hue produced by chemical toning, at once warmer and more precise than any current reproduction, which muddies the design of the lace veil across Swanson's dark hat.) By asserting the beauty of artifice, here and in other portraits, Steichen suggests nothing or very little about the performer's self or psychology or character.

The hatless and tragic Keaton of Clarence Sinclair Bull, an uncelebrated photographer, is more revealing as a "pictorial biography" than any of Steichen's famous theatrical portraits (Robeson as Emperor Jones included), which ought to say something about the shaky circumstances and lacunae of photographic history and criticism, an area as underdeveloped as an average fellow's vision. Self-conscious about his early baldness, the late father-in-law of a friend of mine always wore a hat when he posed for a snapshot, even indoors, never realizing how funny he would look in the family albums, in picture after picture,

the only man with a hat, forever—"Haha, look at grandad's Bogart lid, 'Xmas dinner 1944.' " But such Steichen performers as Von Stroheim, Dietrich, Astaire, Ed Wynn, George Arliss, and Bea Lillie are legitimately and enviably sheltered beneath the assorted headgear of their respective theatrical roles and personae. Grinning confidently, Maurice Chevalier doffs his straw boater gratefully, on behalf of them all. Seldom shot in open close-up, Steichen's theatrical personalities are invariably protected or depersonalized by costumes, stage makeup, multiple exposures, or ripe symbolic props—Notre-Dame for Gordon Craig, the Parthenon for Isadora Duncan, its *stones* retouched by Steichen, who was more beholden to props than a Renaissance painter or Hollywood hack since he didn't like to perform cosmetic surgery. Because his statesmen, writers, and tycoons have no hats to hide under, Steichen has treated them to the unfailing politeness and kindness of soft lights and elegant chiaroscuro. Condé Nast employed him, but Steichen's respectful portraits look like official or authorized releases, except for his much earlier images of J. P. Morgan (1903) and Richard Strauss (1906) and, for *Vanity Fair,* an Expressionistic Eugene O'Neill (1932)—looking too much like Boris Karloff in the previous year's *Frankenstein*—and Henry R. Luce (1935), photographed in a particularly brilliant and clever manner. Steichen's Luce is powerful and prim, but not offensively so—a man of vision as well as a press lord—this equipoise reminding us of the recent past, when the portraits of dignified generals and wise politicians regularly

Edward Steichen, *Gloria Swanson, New York,* 1924.

adorned the covers of *Time* magazine and we believed in the idea of the great public man. It is Steichen who best preserves such sweet illusions, and he did so without recourse to fulsome flattery or vulgar sham. We honor him for his artful discretion rather than his insight. He is the photographer who should have taken our picture of record. No one would laugh at us then. Steichen says the Swanson portrait came about as a kind of gag, an improvisation at the end of a long session, the vamp cast as a leopard in the jungle. What exquisite camouflage you have, grandma! Let's cover our tracks one last time, for the camera, and *then* confront that uncompromising mirror.

Stars enjoy a curious kind of immortality, now more than ever, thanks to TV. Like a highly doctored glamour portrait, the Late Show cancels death and other imperfections. An often repeated TV tribute to Warner Bros. or Bogart includes two flashy montages of numerous clips that show him gunning down the opposition and then being shot himself, each of the climactic visuals and thespian exclamations so similar that they become funny, far cries from the silent and grave commitment of Helen Levitt's street players (p. 89). If one complained to the producer or director that there is something disquieting about seeing a deceased actor die fifteen times in about as many seconds, the filmmaker might reply that it's only reel death, a stylized set of conventions arrayed for laughs, and Bogart is alive and well elsewhere, since cinema is in the present tense (the director has an M.A.). But the deep and lasting appeal of the Bogart character, predicated on our sense of needs and fears masked forever, is not a matter of conventions, and to send it up is to underscore the extent to which our culture is unwilling to "entertain" the idea or ideas of death. *Newsweek* magazine lists deceased notables in a section titled "Transition," as though our sudden passing could be effected gracefully by a slow dissolve, diagonal wipe, old-fashioned irising, or, if we're a star, an extra commercial to give the technicians a chance to change one reel for another—the canned one-hour special which will canonize youthful images of the star, allowing him to achieve instant immortality without having undergone the indignities of mortality, or so it would seem to his fans.

This 1941 portrait of Bogart, by George Hurrell for Warners (right), is as spurious as a "film-bio" on TV. Bogart's famous cigarette, an expressive prop as well as a lethal narcotic, is nowhere in sight, and the metabolism of his attire is too low; the unbuttoned shirt, borrowed from Victor Mature or Jon Hall, is ludicrous where Buster Keaton's was appropriately constrictive, marking *his* chest as a flat and open target. The chair belongs with Ann Sheridan, Joan Crawford, or Dolores Del Rio, and the prissy pose— what *shall* I do with my hands?—is all wrong, since the Bogart character never sits still for long. He's also too far from the camera and the affective potential of the picture plane. By retouching even the famous scar above Bogart's lip, the photographer insists that the middle-aged "tough-guy," age forty-two, is as vain as the next girl. But nature sometimes contributes to our education by rejecting such artifices and postures. Such was the case with my own Bogart, forty years ago, at Woolworth's, where, from about 1942 on, his framed picture was ensconced in the far-left window, next to a demure Turhan Bey, who, like Friedlander's Mickey Rooney, was protected from the shade and dressed to kill. But my informal Bogart, an unlit cigarette in his hand, was grinning broadly, perhaps over the bad taste of his peach-colored sportshirt, which actually suited his permanent place in the sun, a punishing fate for a print in four blatant colors, as each subsequent year proved. (Only the two main front windows were ever changed, for hackneyed seasonal displays of crepe-paper turkeys and cotton snowflakes pasted against the glass.)

George Hurrell, *Humphrey Bogart,* 1941.

By 1952, when I graduated from high school and saw the window for the last time, the frame bore an albino Bogart, a man afflicted by exposure yet hopefully attired in Malibu white—or is that a hospital gown? The confident grin is now idiotic or pathetic; he doesn't see the trouble he's in. The cigarette has been bleached away—white on white, a spectral line, very Style Moderne, Crawford by Hurrell—and, poised in midair, Bogart's empty fingers look funny ... but who is laughing? And if that glamorous portrait is still there, Bogart has faded into nothingness, or Lee Friedlander's dark frame, the deathly picture plane of Richard Avedon's great photograph of Bogart, from 1953, the only portrait of a movie star I ever clipped from a magazine and tacked to my wall, over the protests of my college roommate, who thought it compromised his portrait of Albert Camus peering over his cigarette in the style of Jean Gabin.

Many glamour shots are bad photographs because they do not communicate any sense of the star's appeal; Hurrell's pretty Bogart may even have been used to publicize *High Sierra* (1941). But Clarence Bull's dark Keaton is an exception, and its cognate, Avedon's Bogart, also limns the essence of its star, surprisingly enough, since Avedon the anti-Karsh usually denies his famous subjects their aura, their special myths. The 1953 portrait (right) of Bogart belongs to Avedon's first period of celebrity portraiture, 1948–58, when his findings, as evidenced by his first book, *Observations* (1959, text by Capote) were quite variegated and not yet the expiation of a fashion photographer determined to cast aside every protective veil and distractive prop (Robert Frank, who ought to know, managed to keep his large dog in the picture when he posed for Avedon in 1975). Bogart, age fifty-four, is allowed no cigarette, weapon, whiskers, trenchcoat, uniform, or costume of any kind (Bogart pedants will demur, and cite his bowties in *Deadline USA* [1952] and *The Harder They Fall* [1956]). Equally austere is the basic Avedon setup, derived from such vernacular forms as "folk" portraiture (e.g. Mike Disfarmer), police mug shots, coroner's reports, ID photos, and passports. The Bogart depicted here is no summer traveler, and whiteness once again marks trouble. A stark background is neutral enough in a small bureaucratic photo, but in an Avedon portrait it becomes a cold void or vacuum. Whereas the chair and various shadows in Hurrell's glamour shot of Bogart suggest a studio environment at least warmed by lights, here there is no

depth of field, no working space for the photographer, and only a two-minute supply of air for his subject to breathe, or so it would seem. Closer to the picture plane than Arbus's woman or Steichen's Gloria Swanson, Bogart is being *thinned* before our eyes, an image absorbed by paper as the man is consumed by another chemistry. Bogart died four years after this, in 1957, very bravely it is said, from cancer of the esophagus. He underwent his only operation in 1956, just after the release of what would be his final film, *The Harder They Fall*—an intolerable "irony" or symmetry. But it was apposite that this photograph should first have appeared in the pages of *Harper's Bazaar,* like the death's-head at the feast in medieval works of art. Although Avedon's camera may have discerned the actor's illness in advance of his doctors, the picture is exceptional because it sees through the sardonic persona of that guarded and self-reliant screen character. But this is the man, not the actor, which is to say they are one in their bracing determination to put up a front, *any* front, in the face of the most painful truth, our common condition, the hard fact that makes your mouth run dry and your pulse leap like a trout. If we wish that this photograph were blown up to 60 by 40 inches or projected on the wall before us it's partly because we remember the moment in Godard's *Breathless* (1959) when the small-time hoodlum, played by Belmondo, stops in front of a Parisian neighborhood theater showing *The Harder They Fall,* studies the large icon-like poster of its star, then touches his own curled lip and intones, *"Bogie,"* after which he should have

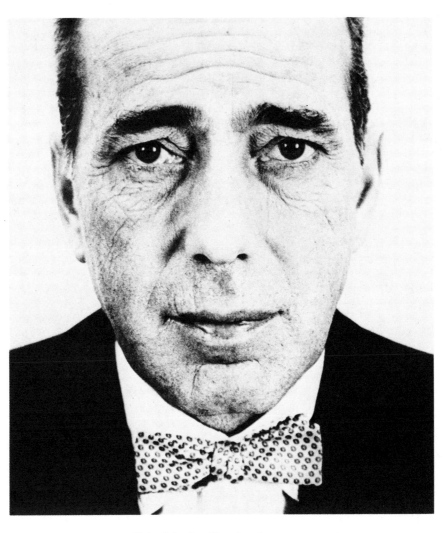

Richard Avedon, *Humphrey Bogart*, 1953.

remembered Baudelaire's "*Mon semblable, mon frère.*"

"Who left this New York *Times* here?" asked the doctor, pointing to (my brother's?) newspaper at the foot of my bed in the Coronary Intensive Care unit. "*Wasser, wasser,*" I thought, remembering the implorations of a dying German soldier in Bogart's *Sahara* (1943). "I did," I answered the doctor, my tongue, thick and swollen, sticking to the roof of my mouth (no water allowed during the first five or six days). "A fellow can't get ahead if he doesn't read the *Times,*" I added. "He's off his head," whispered the doctor, unimpressed by my version of the Bogart mask. The white wall ahead of me started to crack, from lack of sleep, I guess. The cracks spread and began to bleed, but I kept my eyes open till the wall was blank again.

SIGNS OF DECLINE

Ralph Steiner, *Times Square*, 1922.

"Nothing is forever," as a great poet once said, and by glossing a cliché so facetiously, one can see how easy it is for a verbal mask to go awry. But certain subjects nonetheless call for distancing devices, for irony, obliquity, and euphemism. "The painful truth" is one of them. Where most people avert their eyes quickly from the carcass of a squirrel flattened on the street, photographers such as Walker Evans contemplate death in the person of vulnerable and perishable outdoor structures, especially billboards in various stages of decline. By temperament an elegist, a conservator and collector, Evans yearned to preserve his findings by photographing them. He was quite literally a collector, constantly adding to a vast trove of picture postcards depicting distinctive old American buildings and lyrical examples of architectural ephemera, images that complemented his own poetry of the commonplace. Toward the end of his life Evans the conservator-collector would photograph a time-ravaged painted sign and then take it home. Sometimes, reports Jerry L. Thompson in *Walker Evans at Work* (1982), "he would take the sign and not bother to photograph it at all."

Evans's deceptively artless photographic approach to his vernacular subject matter surely owed something to the no-nonsense setups found in antique postcards, real estate photos, and, to move into a less naive environment, Ralph Steiner's sign pictures of the nineteen-twenties. His photo of Times Square (left), contemporary with Irving Berlin's popular song "Always," was taken in 1922, the same year that the painter Stuart Davis discovered "the New York visual dialect" and started celebrating brand-name cigarette packets, disinfectant bottles (*Odol,* 1924), and other disposable objects. *Ulysses,* Joyce's epic of the commonplace, also appeared in 1922; if its perambulating advertising canvasser, Leopold Bloom, had won a jingle contest and free trip from Dublin to Times Square, this billboard would have caught his eye. Bloom is haunted by the suicide of his father and the death of his infant son, and the buckling surfaces or wrinkled skin of *Always,* commerce's *memento mori,* posits the life cycle of a sign. It shouldn't be difficult to read his mind: "Always. Equity. Nothing is forever. Poor papa." Bloom would then have looked away from the billboard and, in an attempt to erase a funereal vision of his dead son, Rudy, dressed up in a fancy velvet suit, he would have thought of something else, possibly the words from a catchy ad or popular song. In the Nighttown chapter, however, Mr. Bloom confronts his demons and ghosts, and doesn't flinch. The photographs of Walker Evans should be studied with this goal in mind. Literature is now in the foreground, paired with unpeopled photographs, a blind date that should offend purists, even those like Tod Papageorge, whose best published picture—New York harbor during the Bicentennial tall ships display of 1976, the crowded scene consecrated by an electronic halo on the central mast (p. 7)—is equivalent to the way Joyce celebrates the ordered jumble of his great, living city.

To most critics and photographers, "literary" is about the worst word one could apply to a photograph. Yet Walker Evans said "photography seems to be the most literary of the graphic arts. It will have—on occasion, and in effect—qualities of eloquence, wit, grace, and economy; style, of course . . . paradox and play and oxymoron." These qualities are abundantly present in Evans's FSA picture, *Atlanta, Georgia,* 1936 (overleaf, right). John Vachon paid tribute to this image by imitating it in 1938, the year that it was published in Evans's benchmark collection, *American Photographs.* Vachon's *hommage* is presented here (right) as a *point de repère,* and the French is in honor of Evans's favorite writers, Baudelaire and Flaubert. Curiously, their names were absent from Evans's short list of writers who "are noticeably photographic from time to time—for instance James, and Joyce, and particularly Nabokov." Evans died in 1975, but had he lived to read Nabokov's last book, *Details of a Sunset and Other Stories* (1976), he would have welcomed "A Guide to Berlin." First published in the December 24, 1925, issue of a Russian émigré journal in Berlin, it is narrated by a nameless man who begins casually enough by entering a pub with his friend and usual drinking companion. "Its sky-blue sign bears a white inscription, *Löwenbräu,* accompanied by the portrait of a lion with a winking eye and mug of beer," says the narrator, whose camera eye fixes quotidian objects for all time.

The sign might have been photographed in muted color by Walker Evans, ca. 1955, for *Fortune* magazine, or in black and white, ca. 1935, for the FSA

and himself—always that, of course, especially if the sign were weathered and peeling, the lion's mug torn in an amusing way, its winking eye direly threatened. "We sit down and I start telling my friend about utility pipes, streetcars, and other important matters," says the narrator, and the locution "important matters" is anything but ironic. Anthropomorphizing the scene, he describes the gigantic black pipes lying on the sidewalk in front of his house as "the street's iron entrails, still idle, not yet lowered into the ground, deep under the asphalt."

In the cold December air, inanimate objects almost quiver with life. It is Christmas, and the narrator cherishes the world around him. As it turns out, he is a scarred and one-armed surviver of the war and, like most of Evans's images—including half of those in *Let Us Now Praise Famous Men* (1941)—his narrative is a meditation on the mutability of things, rather than people. "The streetcar will vanish in twenty years or so, just as the horse-drawn tram has vanished," he says, with eerie prescience, considering the way the Red Army altered the map of Berlin exactly twenty years later, in 1945. "Already I feel [the streetcar] has an air of antiquity, a kind of old-fashioned charm," continues the narrator, whose elegiac mood will take no back seat to Evans's. Even at *Fortune,* Evans remained true to his essential sensibility. "Before They Disappear," a portfolio of old and fading freight-car insignia, photographed in quiet color, is typical of his later "commercial" work (March 1957). Evans's entire mission as a photographer is telescoped by Nabokov's narrator: "I think that here

John Vachon, *Atlanta, Georgia,* 1938.

lies the sense of literary creation: to find in the objects around us the fragrant tenderness that only posterity will discern and appreciate in the far-off times when every trifle of our plain everyday life will become exquisite." Taken as a whole, Evans's work is similar in spirit to the recent spate of illustrated books which try to rescue their respective cities from oblivion. But the relentlessly funereal pitch of *Lost*

New York, Lost Chicago, Lost Boston, et al. should not be confused with the subtle tonal range of a typical Evans photo (see p. 59). A comparison of the two Atlanta images by the two photographers suggests how Evans alone was consistently able to find and emphasize the fun in *fun*ereal, as Nabokov might have said, playing at the edge, a difficult act to follow, as Vachon's picture shows.

The tone of Walker Evans's well-known Atlanta picture from 1936 (right) is easily misunderstood, which is not surprising, since many classics are taken for granted or left unread. John Vachon's 1938 tribute to it (previous page) underscores the exact nature of Evans's accomplishment, and the role played by serendipity as well as talent. "I went around looking for Walker Evans pictures," Vachon said, recalling his apprenticeship as an FSA photographer. "When I'd see an honest-to-goodness Walker Evans in reality it was like a historic find." Vachon walked all over Atlanta until he found these houses; but the result is not a "Walker Evans," because the point of view has been changed for the worse, along with the billboards and several smaller components of the picture. The houses may be on the proverbial wrong side of the tracks, but Evans has included the literal tracks for aesthetic rather than reformist reasons: they anchor a complicated yet elegant network of horizontal, vertical, and diagonal lines made even more cohesive by the frontal view, which minimizes spatial distinctions. The overhead wires complement the trolley lines while the sawed-off trash can commands the pavement from its crowning position atop a diagonal. It in turn is balanced by the washtub on the porch of the house on the left. This compositional exactitude is not a perverse form of dandyism; it expresses Evans's deep respect for the poor but dignified old buildings, the one on the left open to the street, its window neatly curtained, the one on the right closed as tightly as a tomb. The picture's grim aspect is lightened by the middle band running hor-

izontally across it, with its billboard street comediennes. Anne Shirley could be seated on the porch or in the yard, vamping the street or waiting for a specific gentleman caller. Carole Lombard has already received hers, and the resulting black eye is echoed by the architectural oval above her, a delightful surreal improbability, as in Cartier-Bresson. One almost expects her to wink at the camera—*whatta gag!*—whereupon a stentorian voice-over might say that this FSA picture documents the way Hollywood trivialized and unintentionally mocked the plight of people who often enough missed breakfast.

The billboards and houses constitute a contrapuntal arrangement, a blending of pathos and irony akin to the famous country fair episode in Flaubert's novel *Madame Bovary* (1856) when the romantic inanities spoken in the foreground by Rodolphe and Emma are played off against the official event taking place on the platform. "Then there came forward on the platform a little old woman with timid bearing, who seemed to shrink within her poor clothes," writes Flaubert of the worker who receives a silver medal for fifty-four years of service at the same farm. "Something of monastic rigidity dignified her face. Nothing of sadness or of emotion weakened that pale look. In her constant proximity to cattle she had caught their dumbness and their calm. . . . Thus stood before these beaming bourgeois this half-century of servitude." Dumas was no Flaubert, and even his titles won't play, at least not in Vachon. Moreover, *The Count of Monte Cristo* is too foreign a tag to qualify for *American Photographs.* The moonshining

Walker Evans, *Atlanta, Georgia,* 1936.

Ritz Brothers are native enough, but their revelry beneath the open window is too extroverted to be in a Walker Evans. As it is, the ironies in the Evans picture are uncommonly broad for him. Yet Lombard's black eye also works on the viewer in a subtle, associative way, helping to create or imply the consciousness of the dumb structure behind it by subliminally turning the windows into eyes. Its missing plank becomes a major fissure or cut, calmly endured (healed by the time Vachon arrived), and the shuttered window is blind to the street, as Henry James says of Gilbert Osmond's house in *The Portrait of a Lady* (1881). The peeled and weathered remnants of old posters directly beneath the blind window are illegible, of course, yet they represent the handwriting on the wall, an apostrophe addressed to Walker Evans: photograph these things before they disappear.

The tone of photographs such as this 1936 view of Alabama by Walker Evans (right) is often misunderstood by younger viewers who only know the images after the example of the most ironic and sardonic kinds of Pop Art. "When you photograph your billboards, do you do it out of a sense of disdain or derision for them?" a student asked Evans at the University of Michigan in 1971. "Well, I love them, and I'm entertained by them," answered Evans, who could also have been speaking for Joyce, whose *Ulysses* established him as modern literature's premier collector and connoisseur of trash and trivia. Although the ironic newspaper headlines in the "Aeolus" chapter mock cheap journalism, they only represent one specific authorial judgment; Joyce's ad man, Mr. Bloom, remains quite free to savor the city's printed and hand-lettered ephemera, especially in the subsequent "Lestrygonians" chapter, the most reportorial in the book. Here Joyce's documentary eye records the sights of 1904 as evenly and objectively as the camera of Evans or Atget, to move closer to Dublin in space and time. The charm of the observations is sometimes predicated on their *pastness,* their comparative innocence as commercial vehicles: "A procession of whitesmocked men marched slowly towards him along the gutter, scarlet sashes across their [sandwich] boards. Bargains . . . He read the scarlet letters on their five tall white hats: H. E. L. Y. S. Wisdom Hely's [a stationer's]. Y lagging behind drew a chunk of bread from under his foreboard, crammed it into his mouth and munched as he walked." The latter detail is more typical of Robert Doisneau, say,

than of Evans or *Ulysses*'s Lafayette of Westmoreland Street, "Dublin's premier photographer," who took the faded and creased photo of a statuesque young chanteuse in her prime, Molly Bloom, which her sexually blocked husband now carries everywhere, in his billfold. "College sports today I see," notes Bloom, who continually passes professional judgment on the rhetorical and graphic effectiveness of Dublin's commercial signs. "He eyed the horseshoe poster over the gate of college park: cyclist doubled up like a cod in a pot. Damn bad ad. Now if they had made it round like a wheel. Then the spokes: sports, sports, sports: and the hub bit: college. Something to catch the eye." Would Joyce have had Bloom comment on Buck Jones's eye-catching triumph over the Sunny South's Mighty Minstrels? And then remark that such alliterative pairings no longer have the necessary competitive punch? Nabokov would have described the minstrels' visible decline as the spectacle of beauty and elegance caught by time, the pathos of the situation eased somewhat by the camera's X-ray penetration of the villain on the left, a tiger of a fellow who has had bricks for dinner and is—well, the ball is best left undescribed.

Hemingway would have mocked the bogus bravery of a B-movie actor who did in fact die heroically, in 1942, while rescuing people trapped in the Coconut Grove night club fire in Boston. Eudora Welty or the Faulkner of *Sanctuary* (1931) would have used the posters to mark the ascendancy of a meretricious and standardized mass culture at the expense of a regional culture. "Same songs ever'where," com-

Walker Evans, *Posters, Alabama*, 1936.

plains the itinerant Southern guitar player as he listens to a jukebox in Welty's early story, "The Hitch-Hikers" (1938). What did Evans himself want the picture to say? Wrong question, sir. "The photographer is a sensualist," he once remarked. "The eye traffics in feelings, not in thoughts." For publication in *American Photographs,* Evans decided to crop the image (as indicated above), thereby transforming it into a self-contained, non-referential pleasure, like music or dance. In visual terms, the enlarged detail is graphic rather than iconographic. The reverse would hold if Evans had offered a tight shot or cropped version of the pulpy Western poster, a stilted and crowded composition that would inevitably appear to be an ironic piece of found self-parody—an *Ur*-Roy Lichtenstein. As it is, in its published version, the minstrel detail should be perceived warmly as a memento of a turn-of-the-century style of commercial art, barely preserved on a brick wall in Alabama.

Ralph Steiner took this photo (right) in New York City in 1929, and its mordant tone and symbolism have been unwaveringly clear for more than fifty years: this is the way we live in the twentieth century, circumscribed by an ever-rising sea of trash and ephemera. "Thumping thump," thinks Mr. Bloom as he watches the printing presses roll at the outset of the "Aeolus" chapter in *Ulysses,* which follows Bloom in and about two newspaper offices. "Machines. Smash a man to atoms if they got him caught. Rule the world today." If Steiner's photo were a talking picture, its soundtrack would blend the rushing flood waters of *Noah's Ark* with the thumping of the presses; the racket is enough to give a girl a headache, or worse. Let the back lot also stand for the cranial chamber, open to all "media" messages. Indeed, the newborn talkies are already adding their bits and pieces to the visible clutter and confusion; the I in TALKING is about to collapse. JOURNEY'S END is twice announced, as befits the year of the stock market crash. WIN? asks the fragment in the foreground, part of a smashed Winter Garden sign (not everyone will be able to see the question mark). NO! reads the glum, definitive answer. Although Walker Evans allowed that Steiner alone among all photographers might have influenced his work, the even-handed Evans would never have literally slanted a scene this way. Steiner's clear editorial and social angle could well be the result of an editor's request or suggestion inasmuch as the picture was first published in *Fortune,* May 1930, as part of "Vanishing Backyards," a portfolio illustrated by Steiner and the painter Charles Burchfield, decrying the ubiquity of ugly billboards. *Fortune*'s brief text concluded optimistically, but Steiner's view of backyard America is analogous to Tod Hackett's in *The Day of the Locust,* when he contemplates a dumptruck depositing another load on the ten-acre lot given over to discarded movie sets, flats, and props: "He thought of Janvier's 'Sargasso Sea.' Just as that imaginary body of water was a history of civilization in the form of a marine junkyard, the studio lot was one in the form of a dream dump. A Sargasso of the imagination! And the dump grew continually, for there wasn't a dream afloat somewhere which wouldn't sooner or later turn up in it, having first been made photographic by plaster, canvas, lath, and paint."

This is too talky, too ad hominem by recent standards of advanced fiction and photography; what we need now is comic relief. As in most matters, *Ulysses* shows the way, again in "Aeolus." Its one-line newspaper-like headlines gloss the action absurdly, one headline per page, sometimes two, until the last five pages, at which time the headlines start to grow longer and more frequent, crowding the page, almost squeezing out the people altogether, if not smashing them like atoms. The concluding headlines are remarkably funny and timeless because they manage to parody the style of current American gossip weeklies such as the *National Enquirer.* DIMINISHED DIGITS PROVE TOO TITIL-/LATING FOR FRISKY FRUMPS. ANNE/WIMBLES, FLO WANGLES—YET/CAN YOU BLAME THEM? reads the final headline, taking over the page, filling Ralph Steiner's lot to the brim, spillage C.O.D. to S.

Ralph Steiner, *Movies,* 1929.

J. Perelman, whose brilliant sketch "Scenario" (1945) posits a world inundated and overwhelmed by trash, in this instance violent and coarsening movie clichés. "The jig is up," snarls a voice at the end. WHAT RECOURSE? a Joycean headline keeps asking in "Brain Damage" (1968) by Donald Barthelme, our current master of dross. Here headlines hold entire pages captive; the jig is over, save for the authorial performance. "*In the first garbage dump I found a book describing a rich new life of achievement, prosperity, and happiness,*" reads the story's opening sentence. The only recourse is irony, a protective strategy designed to keep at bay the flood of garbage and save us each from drowning.

Like ironic language, the photographer's use of distance is a matter of a delicate balance, the visual equivalent of perfect pitch. Donald Barthelme writes, near the end of "Brain Damage": "*Oh there's brain damage in the east, and brain damage in the west, and upstairs there's brain damage, and downstairs there's brain damage, and in my lady's parlor—brain damage. Brain damage is widespread. Apollinaire was a victim of brain damage—you remember the photograph, the bandage on his head, and the poems . . . Bonnie and Clyde suffered from brain damage in the last four minutes of the picture.*" Even the italics contribute to the tonal balance here. You and I, says the writer, we remember; our cultural brain damage is only partial. We read poems, and remember, and suffer, but at a double remove, at what we hope is a safe distance, like Walker Evans in some of his pictures of pictures. His *Torn Movie Poster, 1930* (right) is as perfectly balanced as the Barthelme passage. If Evans's camera had been farther back, the title of the movie would appear, possibly undermining the affect of the badly torn poster. A close-up of its viscera would be harrowing. The damage before us now is borne equally by the letters and the head, or brain, certainly by the brain and sensibility of Walker Evans, who has turned the poster into an objective correlative for the deepest feelings of a reserved and reticent (dare one say repressed?) man who rarely photographed human displays of emotion. The poster's balance is so delicate that it would be easy enough for a Roy Lichtenstein or Andy Warhol to Pop the image, and drain it of feeling. Imagine a comic strip

balloon above the man's head, exclaiming: "Don't worry, Bonnie, they've stopped shooting!" Pop Art recoiled from emotion, in favor of a truly superficial approach, as in Warhol's various treatments of Marilyn Monroe, which deny her any substance or human dimension. The ironies of the famous *Marilyn Monroe Diptych* of 1962 are arresting, or at least the left-hand portion is, where the twenty-five or so serial versions of M.M. are printed identically in the four blatant colors of a comic book.

The Hollywood duplicating machine rolls on, opines Warhol, who, in making his Monroe silkscreens, has indeed rolled over and subsumed a well-known publicity still, thereby enacting the portrait painter's revenge on photography and the commercial artist's cynical acceptance of the mechanical means at his disposal. With Marilyn's death the presses stop, and the monochromatic right-hand section of the mock-religious diptych is deprived of fleshly colors. The inked images of Marilyn are smeared and streaked, a parody of the work of time, no Luce pun intended. Death is presented as a typographical mess, as though Barthelme had made no distinction between the celluloid brain damage of Bonnie and Clyde and the photograph of the wounded poet Apollinaire. There is a certain imbalance in Warhol, whose pictures of pictures are the antithesis of Walker Evans, even though Evans's most famous picture of pictures—the good-natured *Penny Picture Display, Savannah, Georgia,* 1936, with its two hundred little faces—may have given Warhol his format for Marilyn. When Warhol prints and colors

Walker Evans, *Torn Movie Poster, 1930.*

a scratched negative image of Marilyn (1967) to insist that there is nothing here beyond an arbitrary technical maneuver and a piece of paper, one only hopes that the viewer-reader does not confuse this with the self-conscious art of a Barthelme or, on a higher plane, Nabokov. Ladies and gentlemen of the jury, instead of spray-painting *"Warhol Stinks,"* or worse, on the side of a building, let us agree: brain damage is widespread. *Men of irony, prevail!*

The best-known version of Walker Evans's *Torn Movie Poster* (right) is almost totally unmediated by irony, distance, or the visual equivalent of italic type; only the two letters, pain-free surface phenomena, keep it from being almost unbearable to look at. Taken early in Evans's career and first published in this form in *American Photographs,* the *Torn Movie Poster* is a kind of culminating image, epitomizing the photographer's life-long obsession with signs of decline. It also represents his "full and frank and pure utilization of the camera as the great, the incredible instrument of symbolic actuality that it is," to quote Evans on the obligations of "the seasoned serious photographer." His own "absolute fidelity to the medium" is formulated here by his inclusion of the letters, which make it clear that Evans is not playing any illusionistic games with this poster. The damage may be truly terrible, as symbol or metaphor, but it is not the same as journalistic bad news of the highest order: the bloodied faces and bodies of dead soldiers in the Civil War photos of Timothy O'Sullivan and Mathew Brady, much admired by the youthful Evans. (Modern war photographers invariably avoid the faces of their own dead, as on Buna Beach.) If Evans had wanted to photograph actual corpses, he could have followed Weegee around on his New York City police beat. Instead, he coveted and found symbolic substitutions for death and dying: peeling and weathered surfaces, of course; detritus such as an eerily neat auto graveyard in rural Pennsylvania, where the cars are all facing in the same direction; and various empty rooms, gutted spaces, and abandoned structures, especially a waterfront poolroom in New York (see *First and Last,* pp. 103, 125, 56, and 65). Photographed by Evans at dawn, in 1933, the darkened poolroom looks more grim than Meryon's great 1850 etching of the Paris morgue.

Each of these pictures is equivalent to an old-fashioned *memento mori* or post-mortem photograph, but the photographer's search for them reaches back to tribal avoidance rituals, and the fashioning of taboos and totems that enable the tribe's members to contemplate and learn to live with the unacceptable. Standing alone in his room in 1930, staring down at the freshly developed print of *Torn Movie Poster,* the twenty-seven-year-old Evans may have felt like the Nick Adams of Hemingway's "A Way You'll Never Be" (1933), if only for a few minutes. At the outset of this disturbing and powerful story, a nightmare about World War I, Nick Adams makes his way along a road strewn with the enemy dead, their pockets turned inside out by looters. Unstrung by combat, Nick avoids looking at them, riveting his gaze instead on the debris of battle, especially the personal effects of the fallen—letters, "small photographs of village girls by village photographers," "occasional pictures of children." "There were mass prayer books, group postcards showing the machine-gun unit standing in ranked and ruddy cheerfulness as in a football picture for a college annual; now they were humped and swollen in the grass," writes Hemingway, describing them as though they were corpses. Nick Adams obliquely absorbs the fact of putrescence, confronting "our own dead" two paragraphs

Walker Evans, *Torn Movie Poster II, 1930.*

later: "The hot weather had swollen them all alike regardless of nationality." By the end of the story, he has regained some confidence, and is ready to move on. "I don't want to lose the way [to Fornaci]," he says, speaking for his creator, too. More than one critic has risked intellectual vulgarity and bathos to argue, quite convincingly, that Hemingway's entire oeuvre, his very style, constituted a kind of single-minded avoidance ritual, a necessary and therapeutic activity enabling him to survive. Did pictures such as *Torn Movie Poster* offer such consolations to Walker Evans? The movie poster has clearly suffered a mortal wound, if you grant it its "symbolic actuality" ("SA," if you're in a hurry). Did anyone advancing through the debris yell "Medic! Medic!" when they came upon these two?

Placed here at eye level and framed by the photographer, Lee Friedlander, as though it were a treasured family snapshot, this canceled postcard is at once a *memento mori,* a symbolic substitution after the example of Walker Evans, and a memorial to him (1903–75). Friedlander calls his picture *Cambridge, Massachusetts, 1975* (right), to match the title of the postcard, *Wooden Houses, Boston, 1930,* taken by Evans the same year as his *Torn Movie Poster,* whose mortal head wound has registered on this room, with its diminished or failing vision, its spectral view—the point of view, one may imagine, of a stricken Evans building, about to go down. The Boston image was subsequently published in *American Photographs* and on the dust jacket of the 1962 reissue, by which time the venerable and architecturally charming wooden houses had in fact disappeared, making this postcard appear to be an inevitable conflation of Evans's obsessions as conservator and collector. Such allusiveness is in the manner of Joyce and Nabokov, who have unambiguously evoked, with Hemingway, Wright Morris, and Kafka, our basic call for photographs. "How could you remember everybody?" wonders Mr. Bloom, as he walks through the cemetery at Paddy Dignam's funeral in the "Hades" chapter of *Ulysses,* past gravestones festooned with "Rusty wreaths hung on knobs, garlands of bronzefoil." The gramophone, that's how: "Remind you of the voice like the photograph reminds you of the face. Otherwise you couldn't remember the face after fifteen years," thinks Bloom, as he heads for the glittering cemetery gates at the end of the chapter.

No photographs of someone else's intimate pictorial mementos could be more eloquent than those presented by Wright Morris in his elegiac, photo-text arrangement, *God's Country and My People* (1968), a rare, perfect book of its kind (overleaf, right: an old, flawed mirror reflects its room poorly, the way memory works). Evans's FSA close-up, in *Let Us Now Praise Famous Men,* of a sharecropper's two unframed family snapshots nailed unevenly to the unpainted wooden wall of his shack is equally moving. In one of the cracked and torn photos, an unsmiling old woman stands stiffly, her hands flat against the front of her wrinkled, unironed apron. Her right hand seems to be pulling at it impercepti-

Lee Friedlander, *Cambridge, Massachusetts, 1975.*

bly, as if to make it taut so that she may be photographed and remembered as a neat and dignified person. "Right opposite Gregor on the wall hung a photograph of himself on military service, as a lieutenant, hand on sword, a carefree smile on his face, inviting one to respect his uniform and military bearing," writes Kafka early in *The Metamorphosis* (1915). Although Gregor would no doubt want his family to remember him this way, once they have finished celebrating his death, the photo serves here as documentary proof of Gregor's past strength and wish for paternal command. As an artistic stratagem, it anticipates those advanced contemporary writers who, like the author of "Brain Damage," eschew omniscience altogether and cast their fictions as coolly self-conscious verbal caprices; "objective" compilations of acceptable reports, poems, and letters, "documents" all; unmediated conversations, transcribed from a tape recorder, it seems; first-person narratives and monologues, as in Gilbert Sorrentino's *Aberration of Starlight* (1980), the prototypical contemporary modern novel, which begins with a description and cautious analysis of an unpublished family photo; and various combinations of the above, as in Nabokov, where the playfulness is far from cool, rhetorical masks and ironical distancing devices notwithstanding. "In Kasbeam a very old barber gave me a very mediocre haircut," says the dry-eyed narrator of *Lolita* (1955), whose sense of revulsion makes the passage work like a coiled spring, its human significance released only at the very end, where Humbert the terminal solipsist discovers that there is life on another planet. Humbert continues: "[The barber] babbled of a baseball-playing son of his, and, at every explodent, spat into my neck, and every now and then wiped his glasses on my sheet-wrap, or interrupted his tremulous scissor work to produce faded newspaper clippings, and so inattentive was I that it came as a shock to realize as he pointed to an easeled photograph among the ancient gray lotions, that the mustached young ball player had been dead for the last thirty years."

Wright Morris, *Reflection in Oval Mirror, Home Place, Nebraska,* 1947.

Almost every house and apartment has a family Elysium, a group of photographs arrayed on a mantelpiece or piano, table or bureau. These mementos of the departed are usually framed, of course, and should be kept under glass or it's the end of them, too, their last stand, as in Evelyn Hofer's deliberately pale and muted 1963 *Cemetery Detail, Barcelona, Spain* (right), wherein the deceased child on the tombstone has been photographed next to the Disney dog, Pluto, like a boy king or prince buried with a favorite toy to console him in the spirit world. Photographs function this way in the deepest reaches of our minds, though "our" may only be "me," "my," or "mine"— explosive pronouns each, and especially dangerous to handle when irony has been suspended. As the paramedics hefted me up into the ambulance, a ton of stone pressing on my chest, I imagined that a photograph of my son and daughter had been affixed to the cream-colored, pebble-textured rear wall of the vehicle—a framed double portrait of them as young children, grinning in black and white, uncharacteristic tonalities for this joyful Kodacolor duo, camera-wise at birth, the stars of 1,001 snapshots in uncertain or faded color, who must know with me that monochrome lasts much longer—and then I lost consciousness, regaining it while the Herculean medicos were carrying me into the emergency room. An hour or so later, all hooked up, tested, and medicated, I was left alone for a few minutes—on Mars, it seemed to me. The photograph of my children came to mind again and I focused on the radiant gap-toothed smile of my son, Rockwell in truth, but

the picture did not console me. I was aghast at the very idea of it: why hadn't I thought of them as themselves, as people instead of images? Was it because they were away at summer camp? That sounded good, but the trusting and open expressions on their untried faces flooded my eyes with tears. Several minutes or hours later I rang for someone to ease my thirst. I pressed the call button several times, and finally a nurse rushed in, breathless and apologetic, the front of her uniform spattered with blood. The very old man in the next room had gone wild and ripped the intravenous lines from his nose and arms, the same old man who, throughout my stay, kept calling out, in an unearthly, guttural voice, "moon, moon . . . moon, moon." I wondered what it meant, and so did the nurses, who asked the man's grown daughter when she came down from Wisconsin or Minnesota one day to visit him. She identified it as "Mona," the name of the old man's wife, dead for twenty years. "They are not going to get me this innings," I said aloud, through parched lips, quoting what Bloom thinks as he leaves the cemetery after Paddy Dignam's funeral in the "Hades" chapter. I was not going to need any portable photographic memorials, or become one myself, the grave image in the happy family group atop our TV set, which should be tuned to something winsome and funny rather than anything elegiac or educational—no programs devoted to Walker Evans, certainly, or Wright Morris's vanished Nebraska. Ansel Adams would do, since he sees everything in a good light, tombstones included. Drawing on *Sullivan's Travels* (p. 54) rather

Evelyn Hofer, *Cemetery Detail, Barcelona, Spain,* 1963.

than the aging photo of the pull-toy and child photographed by Hofer, I recommend a Pluto cartoon, or Laurel and Hardy, whose noon-hour reruns I had seen in the hospital once or twice and then watched every day upon my return home, until they were abruptly discontinued. "Too slow-paced for the kiddies raised on *Sesame Street,*" explained the fellow at the TV station when I telephoned to complain. Then I shuffled back to bed again, by the potted plants, *Homo ludens* on sick leave. Where's the *TV Guide*?

SMALL CONSOLATIONS

Laurel and Hardy in *Brats*, 1930.

Small Consolations

Retreat!" is the order of the day, if you bother to decode the simple messages transmitted by the quite recent popular films. Far from being cynical attempts to reduce America to puerilism, "movie movies" such as *Star Wars* (1977), *Superman* (1978), and *Raiders of the Lost Ark* (1981) seem to reflect the needs of at least their adult constituencies. A naturalistic film such as *Saturday Night Fever* (1977) was able to create a dance craze, happily enough, since exercise and human contact are healthy. But the "movie movie," an incongruously grand and self-conscious re-creation of old clichés and conventions, may only inspire the sale of battery-operated toy robots and cartoon T-shirts; human behavior is not the issue. Unlike the best self-conscious (self-reflexive) literature, from Cervantes through Nabokov, the "movie movie" is almost always affectless. The relentlessly swift action of *Raiders of the Lost Ark* keeps the theatre chilled at 46°, better suited to snakes in a pit than to *Homo sapiens*. Lots of characters are killed, but the audience apparently feels no pain. The enormous success of such films is predicated on their bifurcated appeal. Children and adolescents enjoy them as straight action movies, while adults—gradu-ates of the Saturday matinees of the thirties and forties or "kid-vid" hours of the fifties—take delight in the "movie movie" 's campy touches. The humor of *Star Wars* in particular allows a grown-up to exercise his nostalgia at a respectable distance, without having to sink so low as to watch a TV re-run of the inept *Flash Gordon* serial, which is one step removed from sitting on the basement floor with an open carton containing your favorite child-hood toys and memorabilia. The apposite doc-umentary still (left) is from the first scene of *Brats* (1930). Stan and Ollie are playing before bedtime, while their fathers, Mr. Laurel and Mr. Hardy, are completing a game of checkers on the other side of the room. Laurel and Hardy represent *Homo ludens* in his prime, long before the ever-expanding technological universe of TV (cassettes, cable, Home Box Office, video games, and so forth) would seem to have locked most children in. If you look out the window at home, you will notice that the (suburban) street is empty and quiet, even during the summer. This should enable one to sleep late on any given day and to nap at will during the afternoon.

Garry Winogrand, *Hard-Hat Rally, New York, 1969.*

Television is now in command, as movies never were. In an average household, the set is on for six hours each day. By the time a child is seventeen, he or she will have seen 350,000 commercials, and there must be that many specialists studying the almost oceanic pull exerted by the tube. Garry Winogrand is one of them. This picture, *Hard-Hat Rally, New York, 1969* (left), is from Winogrand's *Personal Relations* (1977), part of his project to photograph "the effect of the media on events." On this occasion, the media created the event by turning the clamor of several hundred construction workers into the collective voice of American labor.

Winogrand's wide-angled frame, a dazzling extension of Robert Frank, is as crowded and perfect as an up-tempo solo by Art Tatum or Charlie Parker. Without missing a beat, Winogrand catches the media as it circumscribes its event, from the stolid TV truck parked on the horizon, its crew scanning the field, to the four-pronged thrust being carried out in the foreground by a radio reporter (WMCA), a TV cameraman, a press photographer, and a muffled directional microphone (for movies or TV). The woman on the right, the most anxious person in the photo, is probably a TV reporter (those look like cue-sheets in her hand). She will soon have to supply the words that will make sense of the camera's footage, legitimize it as news. If her crew has shot the central group of hard-hats, she may have missed it entirely. One sympathizes with her, and with those viewers who are too young to read the most overt signs in Winogrand's image, and convert it into history or a personal subjective picture. "The Red May[or]" is John Lindsay, who had just announced his opposition to the Vietnam war. Later in 1969 one million Americans would use Moratorium Day to demonstrate against the war. Yet anyone who remembered the other war at home, 1941–45, and its neatly coordinated flags, was also likely to feel anger, anxiety, confusion, fear, and a concomitant nostalgia; the recent past, a comprehensible entity, began to look better and better. The hard-hats look very bad here, in terms of visual evidence alone. They have placed women and children at the barricades, employed primitive political slander, lost their tempers, and are waving the flags much too wildly, an inversion of *Yankee Doodle Dandy.* According to the Expressionistic tilt of the buildings (upper right), a product of lens distortion, this mob makes the city an unstable and dangerous place. The central group, led by a grotesque Oliver Hardy, could be a deliberate send-up of the 1945 flag-raising on Iwo Jima staged in the spirit of '56, the year that Robert Frank first lowered the American flag and adumbrated the "anti-establishment" mood of the subsequent decade, when chaos seemed to be at hand in even the most enlightened and privileged places (overleaf, left, *New York City, 1971*, an anti-Vietnam war Peace March photographed by Joel Meyerowitz). Concurrent with Jasper Johns's early flags, Frank's mordant and ironic photos of old glory are the first in a line running through Lee Friedlander (1965), Diane Arbus (1967), Robert D'Alesandro (1970; overleaf, right), and such films as *Patton* (1970), *Nashville* (1975), *Smile* (1975),

Joel Meyerowitz, *New York City,* 1971.

and *King Kong* (1976), whose hero, the largest victim yet of the military-industrial complex, begins his New York rampage by ripping down the Bicentennial bunting from Shea Stadium. Anyone who settles for the consolations of irony (Horror Show Amerika Going to the Dogs; above, left and right) or leaps to call the hard-hats beastly has missed the scope of their achievement: they have made the media pay attention to them, and are about to shout their message at millions of viewers and listeners. The crowd on the perimeter of the turmoil is passive and expressionless, as though the event won't exist for them until they can see an edited and codified version on their TV sets. For the little girl in the foreground, TV

Robert D'Alesandro, *Broadway, New York City, Halloween*, 1970.

is the only game in town. She is totally absorbed by the mysteries and spectacle of technology. Can this camera make cartoons? Are there commercials here? How does TV get into our home? The little girl has been granted a rare chance to go behind the seen, to watch if not learn how reality works. Once we have noticed her, she compels attention. She's the future.

Strike through the mask! "Which do you like better, TV or Daddy?" asked a recent survey of children aged four to six. Forty-four percent chose TV. The malevolent spirits in *Poltergeist* (1982) speak to its little girl from the TV screen late at night after "The Star-Spangled Banner" has played and brought the day to a close.

Younger readers who grew up with television rarely have the proper detachment or knowledge of old movies, radio programs, and magazines to see how TV has affected its consumers and competition. If college students were to study the war waged at home by the media, starting in 1941 (p. 11), they would appreciate TV's awesome 1981 victory in Iran, when it single-handedly rekindled American patriotism and heralded the Reagan presidency by raising the flag to its old Warner Bros. heights of 1942–43, when Reagan himself appeared as a corporal in their flag-waving musical, *This Is the Army*. Without TV's overbearing coverage of the hostage crisis, the nation would have lost interest quickly enough. Interest is the key word here. Anyone who aspires to address a "live" audience by himself must contend with the nature of its basic listening experience: TV. A thirty-minute nightly news program presents a different reporter every two minutes or so; the anchorman, that touchstone of "credibility," is on camera for a total of four minutes. Computer graphics enliven every sector of the news, whose producers are nonetheless fearful that viewers will turn the dial; each commercial break is prefaced by a tabloid-style "hook" announcing the subject of the next bit of news (e.g. COMING UP NEXT: LIFE AFTER DEATH? NEW EVIDENCE). One minute of air time is thus deemed to be as long as a week, the gap between movies in one's youth, when the old-fashioned "Coming Attractions" was a capacious form.

Everything on TV is geared to combat boredom and the short attention span, including professional football games, which are narrated gratuitously by three announcers. They are replaced at half-time by a set of "analysts," one of whom is invariably a pretty young woman who smiles the steady starlet smile of the girl in a million ads. And whatever the program may be, the viewer can count on a change of pace every six minutes or so, when the commercials are run.

How, in the face of all this, is one to command and hold an audience's interest and attention? *Star Wars* notwithstanding, the motion picture business has been fighting a losing battle since 1946, successively placing its hopes on 3-D projection; wide screens; Technicolor; violence; sex; sex and violence; special effects; and Dolby sound. When color came to dominate both film and TV, *Time* and *Newsweek* turned to color, too—a paradoxical decision, since it is technically more difficult to control than black and white, and more given to garish distortions and lies. If TV doesn't destroy a magazine or newspaper by drawing away its advertisers, it forces it to become less verbal and more visual; the re-designed page of a solvent publication finds the old printed area broken up into discrete and variegated spatial units, side-bars tinted pink, yellow, or pale green, the graphic equivalent of six minutes of fast-paced air-time, with its different voices, its various pitches.

When *Life* magazine returned as a monthly in 1978 (in color, mainly), it had been scaled down so that its most striking "visuals"—single photos spread across two pages—looked like images on the best available TV screen. Time, Inc.'s *People* magazine (b. 1974), the most successful new magazine of the decade, went

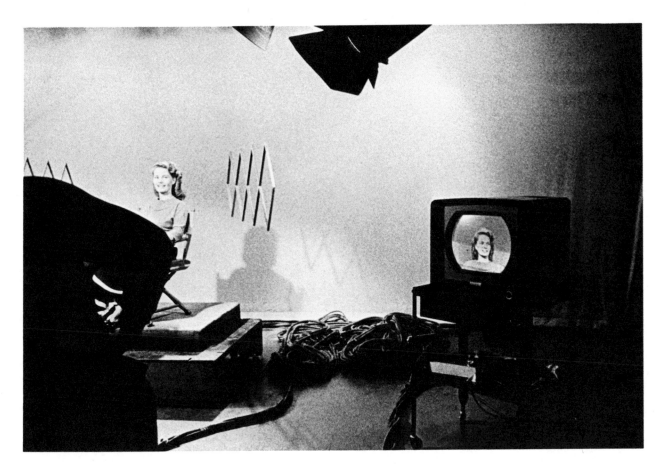

Robert Frank, *TV Studio, Burbank,* 1956.

even further by offering itself as an adjunct to the tube; typically, its cover story is about a TV star, or, like *TV Guide,* it reflects the week's most publicized TV event. Where Henry Luce's old *Life,* for all its fluff, wanted to lead the nation, *People,* its descendant, only follows—like a teenager who wants to be popular. Its editors are "other-directed," to use David Riesman's phrase from the mid-fifties, which was "The Golden Age of [live] Television" (Milton Berle to *Marty*), when Robert Frank photographed this TV studio in Burbank, California (above), for his book *The Americans.* Frank's characteristic grainy graphic fallout persists here, indoors (see

p. 65), recalling the wasteland ashes that drift for miles and settle over everything in F. Scott Fitzgerald's *The Great Gatsby* (1925), furniture included. As a symbol of TV's power, the cable on the floor is equally far-reaching. Professors are aware of it, especially in large lecture halls. Here, unaided by instant replay or a pause in the action, the professor must simply concentrate on maintaining eye-contact with his students, who are accustomed to the perfect delivery of performers who use teleprompters. "You shouldn't look at your script," complained a student, when the course was over; "I didn't realize you were this tall," he added.

TV's spell on America can be documented as easily as the nature of suburban sprawl and certain seasonal vulgarities (Bill Owens took this California interior [right] around 1970, for his picture-book, *Suburbia, 1973*). "I became a passivist during the Vietnam war because of my older brother," wrote a Freshman English student in 1974, in an autobiographical essay. "I dreamed of hitting monmouth home runs in Yankee Stadium, like my idol Mickey Mantle," wrote another student in the same class, his misunderstanding of the sports cliché "mammoth" demonstrating that he too had only heard and perhaps never seen the unmangled word in print. Yes, that's right, that's why the SAT verbal scores are down, because of TV, agreed the high school English teacher on parent's night, after the professor had shared with her his choice solecisms, the best of the worst. In return, she proffered the idiomatic mistake made most frequently in 1974 by sophomores at New Trier Township High School: "Take it for granite." For correlative evidence, one simply turns the dial at random, switching from an old rerun of *Death Valley Days*, say, to something more immediate and relevant. "Name something you do alone," asked the quiz master on the very popular game show, *Family Feud*, 1977. The correct answers, determined by a survey of one hundred people, are "Eat"; "Watch TV"; "Listen to radio"; "Drive a car"; "Sew"; "Type"; and, last as well as least, a very distant seventh in the poll, "Read." The "correct" answer on such shows is solely established by the statistical response of the random control group. Knowledge is never tested.

"Name the people who won't—or didn't—go to heaven," asked the host of *Family Feud* in 1978. Answers: "Nixon"; "Hitler"; "Redd Foxx"; "Burt Reynolds"; "Zsa Zsa Gabor"; and "Dean Martin." The reader should now cover the answer-line below the following question and play *Family Feud* along with the 1977 contestants who were asked to name the most famous Marys in history. Answers: "Mary Hartman"; "Mary Tyler Moore"; "Mary Martin"; "Mary Quite Contrary"; and "Mary Worth." "International Terrorism Comes to Chicago!" announced Bill Kurtis, the local anchorman on CBS, referring to the takeover of a consulate rather than the belated arrival in the Second City of a hot punk rock group. "Let's check the act," said Willard Scott, the jovial weatherman on the *Today* show, as he turned and pointed toward a wide, multicolored "weather map" of the United States. "What's the most popular incest?" a thirteen-year-old girl asked her three friends as they lolled on their bikes outside a suburban ice-cream parlor during Christmas vacation. She had seen a discussion of the subject on that morning's *Phil Donahue Show*. Receiving no reply from her uninformed friends, one of whom was noisily draining a giant malted, she summarized the facts: "Father-daughter incest is most popular. Son and daughter is second most popular. Mother-son is least popular."

After giving a lecture to a large class, around 1974, this sharp-eared and utterly truthful documentarian went across the street to a lunchroom to buy a pack of cigarettes. "Dr. Appel looks younger in person," said one female student to another, *sotto voce*.

Bill Owens, *Ronald Reagan*, ca. 1970.

TV's spell is literally overwhelming, and documentary photographers are not alone in their unwillingness to report any good news about it. Helen Levitt may have been drawn to this 1971 New York scene (overleaf, right) by its striking formal properties—the patterning on the wall, the boy's elegant pose, the play of light on the lowly pipe—but to anyone who remembers another Levitt photo of New York, taken thirty years earlier (overleaf, left), the contemporary conjunction of a bull's-eye and a TV set documents the decline if not death of the spirit of play. The carefully drawn bull's-eye of 1941 is part of a movie-inspired game that must have ranged over the entire neighborhood, but the spray-painted version of 1971 is a youth-gang's inchoate form of self-expression. At best, TV might serve to distract these boys and keep them off the street or at least seated quietly, like all the other passivists.

The Hotel Eden Box #2, 21¼ by 13⅞ by 10½ inches (right), a 1980 construction by the California Post-Minimalist Robert Retla, symbolically compresses a score of jeremiads against TV at the same time that it draws on the actual example of the world's tiniest set, Sony's 4.75-square-inch screen. By alluding to Joseph Cornell's white-walled box-construction, *The Hotel Eden,* with its sublime emblems of imagination and memory, Retla has ironically commented on the impoverished mental sets of his prototypical TV couple, who are further defined by their absence. The word "hotel" is by itself ironic, a reference to the transient nature of subdivision life, where families are always moving in and out of the neighborhood. Vacant domestic spaces are the metaphoric rule in documentary photos ostensibly addressed to the subject of TV. Robert Frank led the way, as usual, in *The Americans,* where TV sets are seen as ironic icons, magical boxes ignored by the apostates; Diane Arbus, Lee Friedlander, and Bill Owens followed suit in the sixties and early seventies, rarely depicting people alongside the TV sets in question. Nowhere in their work can one find an image equivalent to Russell Lee's wonderful photo of the Texas couple seated on either side of their Art Deco cathedral radio, a console in both senses of the word (see p. 24). The film *Melvin and Howard* (1980) shares Lee's sweetness, his sympathetic and uncondescending view of the lowliest sources of nourishment and hope (here, TV game shows).

Cumbersome old Motorola TVs, whether on or off, dominate each cramped interior scene, but life surges and, one might say, Sturges around them, as in Preston (see p. 54). Alas, *Melvin and Howard* isn't a photograph. (In contemporary American literature, Bobbie Ann Mason's *Shiloh and Other Stories* [1982] offers, contra Nathanael West, a rare, respectful view of characters who watch *Charlie's Angels,* craft *Star Trek* needlepoint pillows, and receive counsel and solace from *The Phil Donahue Show,* Ms. Lonelyhearts's successor.)

Among contemporary photographers of any note, only Chauncey Hare regularly depicts people with their TV sets. A representative genre scene from Hare's uniformly forlorn *American Interiors* (1978) shows a morose young woman smoking a cigarette and star-

ing in the direction of a blank TV screen on the other side of her blighted room—which is to say that alienation, more than television, is the subject of these photographers. Their message is clear: modern life is hell. Neither TV nor motion pictures can be expected to renew anyone. And Hell, according to a *New Yorker* cartoon by Richter (June 19, 1978), turns out to be an infernal region where everyone must sit glumly by themselves before their own TV sets, forever. If Frank, Friedlander, et al. had been on assignment for a latter-day incarnation of the FSA, Roy Stryker, their boss, would have sent them a blunt memo: "Can it be that no one in America derives wholesome pleasure from a commercial TV show?" There doesn't seem to be a photographic record of such an extraordinary event, unless we reinterpret Levitt's color photo

Helen Levitt, *New York City,* 1941.

and decide that this young man, his life circumscribed by poverty and neighborhood crime, is receiving some temporary relief by watching the baseball game on the well-camouflaged tube. Retla's construction is in fact a photograph by Bill Owens of an actual interior in California, drawn once again from his book *Suburbia,* and the tag "temporary relief" is from the Rolaids commercial on TV. "Are You Alert Enough to Cope with Today?" (title for a proposed self-help test in a mass magazine).

Helen Levitt, *New York City,* 1971.

The word "documentary" rarely describes the practice of most contemporary photographers of the quotidian. Overwhelmed by the spectacle of all that stuff out there, they retreat, and report bad news only, as in a certain kind of short story. Often they avoid news and events altogether, as in Helen Levitt's recent string quartets (previous page), Joel Meyerowitz's Times Square blast of color (right), and Roy DeCarava's *Coltrane and Elvin* [Elvin Jones, the drummer], *New York,* 1960 (overleaf, left), whose blurry focus and close frame reject reportage and the furious, polyrhythmic essence of their music in favor of earlier, more poetic modes, from Whistler's assortment of London fogs to the dry, floating sound of Lester Young's saxophone. Meyerowitz photographed this vista in 1976, the year he turned from the streets of New York, and the 35mm tacks of Cartier-Bresson, Levitt, Frank, Winogrand, et al., and took his new 8-by-10-inch view camera to Cape Cod, to re-invent the pastoral nineteenth century of the Luminist painters. The result was *Cape Light* (1978), sensibility in the open, about as far as you can get from city life and its concomitant tonal defense systems, its combat fatigue. "Our landlord, Roger Somerset, was murdered last July. He was a kind and absent-minded man, and on the night when he was stabbed there was a sort of requiem for him in the heating system. There is a lot of music in this building anyway. The newlyweds on the third floor play Bartók on their stereo," writes the Valium-popping narrator of Renata Adler's short story, "Brownstone" (1973). At the conclusion of "My Father's Jokes"

(1978), Patricia Zelver writes, "Mother had her pride. I have Literary Tendencies. I am writing this story. Everyone has his or her way of coping." Her voice sounds a dominant chord of the seventies, in prose as well as photography, the self at ground zero, Beckett without the full music, a withdrawn "I" for an eye (see *Prize Stories of the Seventies: From the O. Henry Awards* [1981], where the titles range from "Are You a Doctor?" to "The Dead"). The new color photography can be seen as an eleventh-hour attempt to revive debilitated America by playing big-beat music or plangent chords.

Meyerowitz's unchecked primaries pulsate to *Soul Train* or Dizzy Gillespie here, Elvin on the drums. Bam! You better hold on tightly to your hat—and your portable cassette-radio and little cameras, too, 'cause some dudes are sitting out the dance and the fellow whose face is in shadows sure moves like a pickpocket. When Cartier-Bresson last worked New York, a decade ago, he strapped his Leica to his wrist. To read the full score here, you have to have visited New York and been handed a small advertisement inviting you to one of the neighborhood massage parlors or peep shows. In formalist terms, the outstretched arm of the ad man supports the Carlton billboard, and the festooned pole on the left aspires to Mondrian's painting *Broadway Boogie-Woogie*. But limpid abstraction is more easily within the reach of black-and-white photography, as in DeCarava's *Apartment for Rent, New York,* 1978 (overleaf, right). Meyerowitz was still new to the color beat here. His second book, *St. Louis and*

Joel Meyerowitz, *New York City,* 1976.

the Arch (1980), represents his apogee as a color formalist. Its best images realize Mozart, whereas *Cape Light* sounds like Debussy or Bix Beiderbecke, depending on whether the subject is a windswept bay/sand/sky conjunction or a quietly rejoicing clothesline of freshly washed colors. The more blatant patterns and hues of Times Square are exhilarating nonetheless, and preferable to Winogrand's discordant city (p. 162) and Meyerowitz's dog show. No one is shouting or talking or barking, the volume is up on one tapedeck alone, and the street photographer is out there, "darting and . . . dancing" through the crowd, to quote Meyerowitz on the spectacle of Cartier-Bresson photographing New York City's St.

Roy DeCarava, *Coltrane and Elvin, New York,* 1960

Roy DeCarava, *Apartment for Rent, New York,* 1978.

Patrick's Day parade, 1963. That's *it*? asks a skeptic. That's *all*? Well, yes, but that's not nothing, these days. "It is possible that I know who killed our landlord," says the narrator of "Brownstone," at the end of the story. "Perhaps I do not know. Perhaps it doesn't matter. I think it does, though," she says, writing from her shuttered brownstone. In the context of *Suburbia* and *Interior America,* "I think it does" sounds like a humanist's credo or Billie Holiday near the end, when she managed to sustain her vibrato on the difficult first syllable of "Yesterdays."

This composition, *Coronado Street, Los Angeles,* 1975 (right), by Stephen Shore, is aided considerably by the tree/pole vertical axis on the left, a much imitated Walker Evans device (see pp. 7, 39, 59, 162, 175). The image is typical of Shore, William Eggleston, Henry Wessel, Jr., and Tod Papageorge, who try to see their mission simply and purely in the formalist terms of modern art—Walker Evans without the charm or pain, Roy DeCarava's *Apartment for Rent* caught in full daylight, preferably in color. Sometimes these younger formalists fail, thank goodness. "A photograph of something is not the thing photographed," states Papageorge, who cannot prevent heretics from valuing his wonderful slice of 1976's Operation Sail as a distillation and symbol of the spirited whole (p. 7). Shore's "elegant fields of colored light [may be] immaterial in the real world," as Maria Morris Hambourg says, but this house looks like a certain kind of house, a documentary real-estate record made in the general neighborhood of Raymond Chandler and the movies which he and Hammett have inspired, ranging from *film noir* adaptations of their novels to *hommages* in color such as *Chinatown* (1974) and *The Late Show* (1977). Written and directed by Robert Benton, *The Late Show* stars Art Carney as a sick old Los Angeles private eye who doesn't even own a car. A network of allusions places him in the Great Tradition. The first scene in his shabby apartment features a framed photo of Martha Vickers, who played the psychotic deb in Howard Hawks's 1946 version of *The Big Sleep,* which starred Bogart as Chandler's knight-errant, Philip Marlowe. Hawks's war movie *The Dawn Patrol* (1930) is flickering on the Late Show when Carney's mortally wounded ex-partner, played by Howard Duff (radio's Sam Spade, ca. 1946), topples into the room, like the dead merchant seaman in *The Maltese Falcon* (1941), which starred Bogart, of course, whose photo is conspicuous on the bilious green wall of a restaurant in *The Late Show* just before Carney and his weirdo client, Lily Tomlin, fall under gunfire. As in *The Maltese Falcon,* the private eye feels obliged to solve the murder of his ex-partner, and even a poorly educated viewer who has missed the allusions should be able to see that *The Late Show* is a rare bird among "movie movies": it affirms the content, the ethic of the old genre it questions. Yet Benton makes it clear that the Hawks-Hammett-Chandler ideals of honor and courage and fair play belong more to the realm of popular mythology than life, and he underscores his point by having the movie turn in upon itself at the end, like an involuted modern novel, a self-reflexive artifice whose "reality" ebbs and dies before our eyes. In the last scene, Carney and Tomlin are the sole mourners at a barren locus whose gate proclaims it to be the "Hollywood Cemetary" (sic). They leave and wait for a bus, facing the camera. The bus arrives from the right, filling the screen, stops briefly, and moves left, off the screen. Carney and Tomlin are now gone, vanished, removed from the frame by a diagonal wipe, an old movie convention. HOLLYWOOD WAX MUSEUM/MINGLE WITH THE STARS, reads an ad on the bench on which they had been seated. It also bears a picture

Stephen Shore, *Coronado Street, Los Angeles,* 1975.

of Karloff as Frankenstein, the most famous makeup job of the thirties, when Hollywood and the house on Coronado Street were in their prime. Attracted by the fresh vermilion paint, a platoon of Munchkins might well have rented this place while they were filming *The Wizard of Oz* (1939) or *The Terror of Tiny Town,* a 1938 Western with an all-midget cast. The house is a dolled-up runt, Minnie Mouse wearing Aztec Red lipstick and Frederick's of Hollywood false eyelashes. "Hey! Low blows! Lay off! That's hitting below the house's belt," as Philip Marlowe would say, if he were here, and he'd be right.

Even as it documents a regional style of kitschy architecture, Shore's photo attests to the dream, the consolation of having your own house and land, however small they may be. Built low to the ground, this sturdy bungalow should be the envy of the neighborhood whenever there's an earthquake in town.

Photographs such as Henry Wessel, Jr.'s dispassionate wide-angled view *Hollywood, California,* 1972 (right) and Gene Oshman's *Canadian Club,* 1974 (overleaf, right) realize a formalist's wish to avoid the documentary style and content of the genre's past masters, from the FSA to Robert Frank. Wessel here asserts an aesthetic impulse even more austere than Walker Evans's. While Wessel's composition evokes Evans's famous image of the Atlanta billboard (p. 143), its content marks an affective dead end, keeping the viewer out of the picture. The building is a movie studio, probably Paramount Pictures, but who's to know? By withholding such information from the caption, Wessel neutralizes the "Stop" sign's editorial potential. Even Edward Weston, the most uncompromising formalist of the thirties, went behind the walls of several studios, and expressed his opinion (p. 25). Wessel (b. 1942) is satisfied by the splendid surface of his ostensible subject, and has photographed it as though it were one of those mesa or canyon walls favored by William Clift (b. 1944), one of the few photographers of their generation who still responds to landscapes with the awe of an Ansel Adams (b. 1902). Oshman (b. 1958) makes Times Square equally splendid, seen here from a vantage point opposite Meyerowitz's position (p. 175).

Unlike DeCarava's double-edged title sign, *Apartment for rent* (a living space and an aesthetic coordinate), the title *Canadian Club* refers to an artistic choice alone, the compositional highpoint of a picture. It underscores, in the spirit of classic modernism, the artist's self-reflexive sense of his power to make anything beautiful, from Picasso's Cubist painting "*Ma Jolie*" (1911) and Matisse's painting *The Red Studio* (1911) to William Eggleston's untitled 1972 color photograph of a lustrous, green-tiled shower-stall—a last grasp at high modernism. ("Last gasp," says the self-reflexive narrator of a Beckett-like work, recoiling in parentheses.) Robert Cumming (b. 1943) is remarkably forthcoming with the kind of old-fashioned caption information that allows a picture to work on many levels. His 1977 photo (overleaf, left), from his series, *Studio Still Lifes,* is titled *Gap between Set and Painted Backdrop, TV Special, "It's a Wonderful Life," Stage #12, Universal Studios, Calif.* The name of the show (soon changed to *It Happened One Christmas*) identifies it as a remake of Frank Capra's 1946 movie, a classic American exercise in nostalgia and populist optimism. The snows of yesteryear are now doing a thriving business, from Norman Rockwell anthologies and "collectibles" to Ansel Adams. Could they also be shooting bogus Ansel Adams winter landscapes here? Cumming's gap formulates a wide range of legitimate fears. If illusion is universal, everyone must watch his step and never trust his eyes completely. Often enough the street photographer has said that he doesn't know what he has shot until he's studied his contact sheets.

The photographer is at or close to ground zero, looking for small consolations, and so is the reader, especially if he believes that Gene Oshman took *Canadian Club.* The title is correct, and Oshman exists, but it is in fact a 48-by-60-inch oil painting by the Photo-Realist Richard Estes (b. 1936), another

Henry Wessel, Jr., *Hollywood, California*, 1972.

Robert Cumming, *Gap Between Set and Painted Backdrop, TV Special,* from *Studio Still Lifes* portfolio, 1977.

admirer of Walker Evans. Times Square might have looked this immaculate in 1944, but never in 1974, when Estes painted it in his Maine studio, working from a batch of photographs. Unlike Rockwell and several Photo-Realists, who copy photos slavishly, or the Pop artists who mimic them ironically (Rosenquist, Mel Ramos), Estes edits and revises his photographic sources to help him reconstruct a subtly better place. The 76° temperature on the Coca-Cola sign is perfect for people if not soft drinks, though the city is as still and unpopulated as Adams's Yosemite Valley or one of Edward Hopper's urban pastorals. Curiously, the refuse in Wessel's actual gutter is more

stylized than in Estes's canvas, which in every other respect is a fantasia, a dream-perfect set quite removed from Winogrand's city. The only proven gap is in the mind of any reader who has failed to see that Estes's "photographic" painting is a multiform construct, an exhilarating optical utopia comprised of numerous crystal-clear focal points and planes that are quite beyond the capacity of any single lens or pair of eyes. If you were tricked twice in this section you had better take a leave of absence, sell some of your signed Ansel Adams prints, and stay indoors from now on beneath a roof as tightly capped as the one photographed on Coronado Street by Stephen Shore.

Contemporary avant-garde photography is often as self-reflexive as modern art, film, and literature. "My pictures are about color," says William Eggleston, whose shadow is visible on the edge of this roof in Greenville, Mississippi (right). Rear-guard photographers act this way, too, if only once. Liliane De Cock's *Ansel Adams* (1972), the best medium-priced collection of his work, and the only one that will fit on a night-table, concludes with a 1958 shot of the photographer's shadow caught in action on a canyon wall in Monument Valley, Utah. His arms are raised high, as though he were conducting and creating Nature, which in a sense he is, unless you think that you can find an "Ansel Adams" by simply driving your camper into Yosemite on a clear day. If Adams's shadow best represents the imperial self in a most enviable position, then Lee Friedlander's self portraits (he omits the hyphen) are definitely the pits.

Idiomatic lingo suits a range of pictures whose drab and depressing quotidian environments at once question the ambiguities of space and complement the dark moods of Friedlander, who variously casts his shadow or reflection in each of them. "FVCK," it says, in large white letters, spray-painted below an oval mirror on a bare dingy pasteboard wall photographed by Friedlander in 1966. His little face is barely visible in the mirror, a loser's version of the most famous picture of this kind, Van Eyck's *Arnolfini Wedding* (1434). The otiose Latin *U* suggests Juvenal graffiti, or a history lesson by Mel Brooks addressed to and proving the long decline of everything. What recourse? Answer: small jokes,

ground-zero humor. Henry Wessel thus offers literal examples of stunted growth, sun-drenched anti-landscapes depicting palm trees that are too skinny or too squat, and a palm sapling that looks like the planted trunk of a baby elephant. Wessel's picture of a distant range of low-lying mountains in Utah is elegantly composed, but this nature photographer's long and rigid shadow is restricted to the edge of the highway, next to a larger hulking form (his camper?), stressing his tourist-like distance from the idea of a beautiful mountain, and the pantheism of an Ansel Adams or Eliot Porter (b. 1901). Eggleston's color close-ups of trees and flowers refuse to be pretty, his way of cutting down Porter's use of color and the Nature idea (see *American Images,* pp. 81–88). Eggleston is anything but distant from this Mississippi roof, photographed around 1976, an especially remarkable picture if one is familiar with his controversial collection, *William Eggleston's Guide* (1976), which presents a bleak vision, in color, of ordinary life in the contemporary South, its newly installed green shower-stalls notwithstanding. The bemused men who slump or stand alone in their Mississippi rooms look like potential suicides, and Eggleston casts his shadow in the local cemetery (his family's?). The emphatic PEACHES sign, however, has given him a lift, making him clamber up on this roof, like Ansel Adams assuming a boulder. It is as though Adams had decided to make a potential Walker Evans picture his own (see p. 59), omitting any information about the rest of the structure. For the moment, the roof is a corrugated Art Deco landscape, patently "authorial" since

William Eggleston, *Greenville, Mississippi,* ca. 1976.

only the photographer can see it this way. Is Eggleston (b. 1939) trying to re-enter his nineteen-forties Mississippi boyhood, like Wright Morris, who in 1947, in the course of elegizing his vanishing Nebraska, had cast his shadow in front of a Model-T Ford? This sounds sentimental, and, since sentimentality is the most dreaded critical disease, let us rescue Eggleston by noting that his shadow is small enough so that he should be able to get off this roof easily and then go into the country store below. But as the warped screen door slaps shut behind him and he feels the old floorboards give beneath his feet, his heart will skip a beat and he'll wish he were nine again so he could buy an icy Coke, borrow the new *Terry and the Pirates* Big Little Book from the notions counter, sit down on the floor against the wall, and stay here forever. At worst, boys playing Kamikaze Attack will occasionally speed by on bikes and try to hit the roof with small stones, Mississippi hand grenades. What a bad noise!

Like the nostalgist who tries to confer a deathless glow on the past and its lowliest artifact, Ansel Adams has consistently captured the sublime, or at least succeeded in putting a good face on a failing structure (right, his 1938 "fadograph of a yestern scene" [*Finnegans Wake*] in Bodie, California, soon to become a ghost town). Although nostalgia is often a sentimental impulse, many of the rescue operations performed in its name are also worthy enough, and easily explained. The violent, coldly perfected special-effects of contemporary films send viewers back to the warm if artificial winters of yesterday, turning *It's a Wonderful Life* into a latter-day *Christmas Carol.* The bland invulnerability of tight-lipped Clint Eastwood seems to transform the slightest quiver of Bogart's upper lip into a paragraph by Hemingway. The impersonal and boxy glass skyscrapers erected during the last two decades have made the ornamental Art Deco style of the past look even more sensuous than it did in its prime, long before it had become a respectable academic area and a subject for picture-books. Industrial pollution and art's Return to Realism have made some of Grant Wood's folksy Art Deco landscapes look good again.

The utilitarianism of contemporary automotive design has helped to turn the most handsome cars of the twenties and thirties into "classics," and they are photographed in idyllic rural settings, but so are the cars of 1956, the same ungainly tail-finned jobs that Robert Frank's glum Americans once tooled around in so aimlessly. Must *everything* now have its day in the sun? What's going on here? As the future grows more problematical, the past, or myths about the past, grow more precious. Vintage toy airplanes, Mickey Mousiana, and the magic rings and decoder badges bestowed by radio shows are coveted by adult collectors who will pay high prices to own what others may only view in Time-Life's sixteen-volume *Encyclopedia of Collectibles* (1978), where such items have been photographed in lustrous color as though they were the treasures of Tutankhamen. Nostalgia, to be exact, means "homesick," and that emotion can sanctify most anything. Witness *The Last Convertibles* (1979); *"Fill 'er Up": An Architectural History of America's Gas Stations* (1979); *California Crazy: Roadside Vernacular Architecture* (1980); *Jukebox, The Golden Age* (1981); and *The End of the Road: Vanishing Highway Architecture in America* (1981), recent picture-books that lament the passing of machines, one-of-a-kind motels, diners, and so forth.

The standardized fast-food restaurants of today are admittedly a depressing spectacle, but most of these picture-books try to give the Walker Evans treatment to the sort of roadside kitsch that he would have scorned and ignored, at least until the last two years of his life, when he took to making color shots of bright old Dairy Queen frozen custard logos much like the ones memorialized in *The End of the Road. Crazy California*, devoted to the bizarrely shaped buildings once mocked by West, Perelman, and Nabokov, concludes with an elaborate map to the twenty-five structures still standing, from the famous Brown Derby down to the Big Donut and the Chili Bowl.

Ansel Adams, *Bodie, California,* 1938.

These books are delightful as social history, but the author-photographers seem to be after something else—the Big Donut as Rosebud? Even color photography fails to elevate most of the structures in *The End of the Road,* with the definite exception of a splendid picture of Dick's Motor Inn in Banning, California. The photographer, John Margolies, has caught the warming brilliance of early morning sunshine on the pale pink stucco walls of a closely grouped row of cabins. Behind them, the softly rounded snow-capped peaks of the low-lying San Bernardino mountains glint under a cloudless cobalt-blue sky, as though man and nature were being equally blessed. As the paramedics swung me around behind the ambulance they paused to make some sort of adjustment and, in that instant, as the swaying oaks and elms above me held still, the stretcher seemed to levitate, and I framed and memorized three or four branches of sparkling leaves, producing a rare and valuable Ansel Adams color Polaroid of my own.

In the face of chaos and darkness, we assert our will and strive to hold on to light, in all its manifestations. Jerome Liebling's 1977 photo of the New York neighborhood once photographed by Helen Levitt (right) imparts this well: the graffitist's "Bogie" at street-level, the insomniac's night-light above. From my hospital bed I was able to look out the window throughout the day, starting at dawn, and follow the progress of the dark treetops below as the sun animated their various aspects. TV discharged another kind of welcome light, especially late at night when I was reluctant to close my eyes and would hold off the effects of Seconal as long as possible by watching almost anything on TV except extended fistfights, long-distance Olympic runners panting for breath (this was the summer of 1976), and sudden "newsbreak" pictures from NASA's space probe Lander on the surface of Mars, whose pebbles and duststorms looked to me like the particles of dead professors. Home from the hospital but now distracted by angina, I prepared for the night by perusing either the 1930–40 volume of Time-Life's *This Fabulous Century* (1970) or Ansel Adams, especially his less dramatic images of crystalline summer grasses, snow-rimmed black branches, groves of slender white aspens, and mountain streams and meadows glowing at dawn. If Estes's book *The Urban Landscape* (1978) had been available, with its Arcadian Times Square—Luminism for Post-Moderns, and quite safe for grazing—it too would have been prescribed. It offers no less than Adams the restorative promise of traditional pastoral: "Tomorrow to fresh woods, and pastures

new." *This Fabulous Century 1930–1940* offered an unaccredited course in an adjacent field. Its twenty-page "Dream Factory" section is truly fabulous, reproducing in honest color the items that were once astonishing to a child: Buck Rogers ray guns, a Ralston Straight Shooters's chart detailing "Tom Mix's Injuries," and the secret-code cards, rings, and badges that allowed the radio followers of Captain Midnight, Little Orphan Annie, and Jack Armstrong to decode messages that partly revealed the next day's installment. My favorite page in the section contained Jack Armstrong's chart-game *Adventures with the Dragon Talisman,* an illustrated treasure-route map of Asia. More than once I turned out the light only after looking hard at this map. I realize now, six years later, as I write, that it resembled *Native Means of Transportation in the Pacific Area,* one of a set of four splendid maps by the Mexican artist Miguel Covarrubias. It hung on the wall near my pillow when I was six years old. Each evening, seasonal light permitting, I used its little pictures as starting points for happily resolved adventure stories starring me. Like the Jack Armstrong map, it depicted almost every form of indigenous locomotion, from elephants to sampans, and the entire Pacific area was commanded by that 1939–40 touchstone of aeronautical glamour and adventure, Pan Am's streamlined "China Clipper"—"The Shape of Tomorrow," as Style Moderne was then referred to. So-called nostalgia seems to work for some as another form of pastoral. BUTTON TO/SECRET PASSAGE/PRESS, to quote the graffiti photographed by Helen Levitt at about this time.

Jerome Liebling, *Casablanca Meat Market, E. 110th Street, New York City,* 1977.

Many adults have returned again and again to see *E.T., The Extra-Terrestial* (1982), a childhood pastoral; the elfin visitors from outer-space are here to gather mushrooms, and they alight from a spacecraft that looks like an old-fashioned Christmas tree ornament—The Shape of Yesterday. Yet nostalgia is a palliative, not a cure. One night, after absorbing Adams's Yosemite, I dreamed that I was walking alone to the Playhouse to catch the early show on a warm Sunday evening. I stopped short on the tree-lined side street by the theater because its four exit doors had been boarded up. The fire! I keep forgetting. I hurry by, averting my eyes from the (scorched? destroyed?) marquee, and head up the street to see if there are any good games going on in the school playground. The sun is up by the time I get to my usual short-cut, a rent in the back fence. But it's been boarded-up, too, and I start to cry, and dash along the fence, searching. Now I'm awake, and tears are coursing down my face. Horrible. What a big baby!

Lee Friedlander, *Galax, Virginia, 1962.*

Most of the fare on TV is no doubt pablum, and it may stunt the growth of many consumers, but it also provides sustenance for adults whose backs are against the wall, literally so here, in Lee Friedlander's *Galax, Virginia, 1962* (left). On the road, lonely, down, the photographer watches TV; seeing an image on the tube that somehow corresponds to his mood, he reaches for his camera and snaps this picture. The baby is truly larger than life, the way TV often appears to the aged, the ill, the infirm. At one a.m., the bedridden neighbor across the street is still watching TV in his upstairs room, as he does every night, the screen facing us through his open window. On this particular moonless night the wall of total darkness seems to thrust the incandescent object forward, as though it were a sci-fi visitor bearing an urgent message—Galax Express?—or the riveting night-light in our open closet or hallway when we were young and feared the deep shadows under the bed and Monstro the whale, who had swallowed Pinocchio whole— hey, keep the light on!—which returns me to my hospitalization, and the tiny TV set that was suspended above my bed, along with the oxygen and intravenous paraphernalia. Certain unlikely shows were most sustaining: *The Blue Knight,* a mawkish cop show in which every Damon Runyanesque low-life in the neighborhood had a dog or friend; *Ellery Queen,* set in the nineteen-forties and notable for the way the father and son detective team fixed soup together in their little kitchen while it rained outside; Laurel and Hardy, as their own fathers in *Brats,* tucking themselves in for the night, thanks to trick photography; and *Wild, Wild World of Animals,* especially their program on beavers, narrated by William Conrad, a stalwart radio voice from the forties (Marshall Dillon of *Gunsmoke*). Beavers, I learned, can remain underwater for fifteen minutes without air. They are monogamous for life, loyal and loving as well as clever. The TV program showed how they build their dwellings in the spring, divert the flow of streams and rivers to accommodate their system of entranceways and passages, teach their young to swim, guiding them underwater with pushes and nudges down into their underground nest beneath the pond, now frozen, the TV camera there, able to present the beaver family on the home screen, curled up in its fortress, unfazed by ice and snow or predators, like Pinocchio reunited with fatherly Geppetto in the belly of the whale, where they make cozy good use of some undigested furniture and an incandescent candle. As I drew deep breaths, easily, unhurriedly, I remembered my boyhood room, where on winter nights I would sometimes turn off the light during a blizzard, stare at the snow through the window, briefly try to count the largest snowflakes afloat in the middle distance—*Dick Tracy* snowflakes, drawn by Chester Gould, as large as snowballs—and I touch the cold pane and savor my sense of security. Friedlander's TV baby is at the foot of the bed, like the cradle in a colonial American family—an excessive or extravagant simile inasmuch as the past is a good area to visit but a dangerous place to dwell, or so we are told, and sometimes discover for ourselves when its figures or figments crowd around and take up too much room, call it nostalgia or the pastoral (right, a 1942 convocation of characters drawn by Milton Caniff from the childhood of *Terry and the Pirates,* b. 1934). What's on tonight? I asked myself, wanting something to look forward to as I awoke from my daily nap late one afternoon during the Arctic Chicago winter of 1977, following my hospitalization. I was still on sick leave, staying indoors, depressed, watching more TV than ever before—even game shows, and old animated cartoons and *Flash Gordon* on Saturday mornings, the screen a vague daydream of a vibrant Playhouse Theatre. It was very dark in the room. What's on? What night is it? Wednesday . . . Oh, good, *Mr. Keen,* at eight o'clock. "Oh, my God!" I said as I reheard and recognized the title of the nineteen-forties radio detective drama, *Mr. Keen: Tracer of Lost Persons.* My wife and thirteen-year-old son hurried into the room. "What's wrong?" she asked. "I thought it was 1944," I answered. "Let me tuck you in again, okay?" said my son.

Milton Caniff, a group portrait from *Terry and the Pirates,* 1942. Original picture in color.

Come out, Laury!" called my son, age three, as the curtain closed over the big screen and the lights came on at the conclusion of his first picture show, a revival of *Babes in Toyland* (1934), starring Laurel and Hardy. "Watch out, Laury!" he had cried out earlier, as the boys entered the vast subterranean chambers of bogeyland, its hairy monsters concealed behind immense stalagmites and boulders. Although my son had seen Laurel and Hardy on television many times, he'd never addressed the tube directly. His definition of the cinema's special aura also pinpoints the vital nature of popular images absorbed years ago and stored somewhere in our minds as though they were memories of actual experiences and events. Early one morning during my convalescent winter at home, a time when slumber was being ruined by as many as five horrific dreams each night (Freud's repetition compulsion, I could tell myself; orthodox, classic stuff), I was visited by a large man wearing a camel's hair coat, matching cap, and carrying a generous bouquet of flowers. "Babe!" I exclaimed, recognizing George Herman Ruth as he stepped up to my hospital bed, into the spotlight, and looked down at me and my array of lifelines and wires. "Hey, Babe, let's go out and hit a few," I said. "Hey, keed, you're alright," he answered hoarsely, and I saw that his shining eyes were sunk in deep shadows. Grinning, he whipped off his cap, drew a straw boater from the bunch of flowers, and smashed it down over his head. I was awakened by my own laughter. I explicated text and image: straw hat courtesy of *Pride of the Yankees,* revised by me, of course, but I couldn't remember if Ruth had visited the dying Gehrig in the latter movie or several years later in *The Babe Ruth Story* (terrible movie). Hadn't Gary Cooper, as Gehrig, visited a wretched Dickensian sick boy in his hospital room and promised to hit him a home run that afternoon? The voice, the eyes—they were from 1948, Yankee Stadium, the ceremony marking its twenty-fifth anniversary, where the Sultan of Swat, the immortal Bambino, soon to die of throat cancer, had suited up for the last time and, hunched over the microphone at home plate, had whispered farewell to the fans, the rasping tonalities of his ruined voice making the public address system crackle and pop. I had heard the ceremony on the radio and seen it in newsreels two or three times, his sunken eyes lost in twin caves, especially in murky newspaper photographs, which also emphasized the way he leaned on his bat, scepter as cane.

The explicator and lay diagnostician were amazed and impressed by the dream, as though it were a little playlet planned and executed perfectly by some anonymous cranium-based mental healer, the least expensive therapist. Did the dream really signal a break in the weather? How does the mind work? Would the burnt-out Playhouse be re-opening soon for business? Do old video images make house calls? Deliver flowers? Along with unpopular culture— words and images provided by Joyce and Nabokov, Baudelaire and Milton—Milton Berle? No, no, not yet—the playhouse spirit did send the sick boy out to walk if not dance in the street, which returns us to where we began (1942 and *Yankee Doodle Dandy*)

Ernst Haas, *Petroglyphs, Canyon de Chelly, Arizona,* 1971.

and, before that, the uphill course and durable playground of the mind depicted in this 1971 photograph by Ernst Haas (above). These petroglyphs, the earliest signs and symbols of life in America, were painted in the Canyon de Chelly, Arizona, several thousand years before Helen Levitt photographed the more verbal wall art of the New York School.

Although Eastern mystics see the bull's-eye or archetypal mandala as their passage into the depths of the mind, its meaning(s) is (are) still quite debatable. The two stylized fellows, evidently antic and frightened hunters on the run, must be the Laurel and Hardy of their set, preserved on the wall to make cave-dwellers laugh whenever they are under the weather.

A Walk in the Neighborhood

S tan and Ollie!" exclaims the photographer, almost stumbling over these two boys. "Great! Hold it! Smile!" The woman on the right is also delighted by their appearance, and so are we, especially by the fact that Laurel and Hardy are wearing berets, like everyone else in Paris, where this untitled photograph was snapped by Elliott Erwitt in 1949 (right). Perhaps the two boys have just received the masks as gifts or prizes from their neighborhood cinema; their berets and high-necked collars certainly make the masks seem more facelike than they should. If a preoccupied pedestrian were to hurry across their path, he'd do a double-take, and smile: these boys have realized the most dire warnings of the Payne Fund Studies of the nineteen-thirties (You Are What You See). They've turned into Laurel and Hardy, which isn't the worst possible enchantment (boys into donkeys in *Pinocchio*) since it should make them gentle and sweet-tempered, optimistic and patient. The other woman bestows an uncommonly trusting smile on that aggressive predator, the street photographer; she's also in a Laurel and Hardy mental set. No one wants to strike through the mask here. To be sure, the masks are caricatures, and the dwarfish Hardy boy isn't up to scale, but it doesn't matter; the masks stand for the comedy team, and their motion pic-

tures. Erwitt's still photo achieves in turn an almost cinematic dynamism. Its shallow focus, angle of vision, and foreground cropping propel the boys toward us, like the masked and costumed children setting out on Halloween afternoon in *E.T.,* the title character wobbling from side to side among them, and the trick-or-treaters coming down the street in our neighborhood, also in the afternoon (since the nights are now dangerous in every suburb). The children are pouring out of their houses, and fanning out through the neighborhood, tripping along in their large webbed space-creature feet.

On every other day, however, except for the Fourth of July, the streets and lawns and backyards are quite empty, confirming the view from sick bay. No one uses the well-equipped playground or athletic fields of the neighborhood grammar school. A pair of uniformed Little Leaguers bike by on their way to the municipal park. Men are mowing their lawns on Saturday morning up and down the block, unassisted. The cultural critic wants to look through the sturdy walls of their houses, into their "rec rooms" and dens, where the children must be watching TV. Are they also playing, and talking with their siblings, and hugging their pets, and drawing pictures, and read-

Elliott Erwitt, Untitled, Paris, 1949.

ing William Kotzwinkle's nice *E.T.* spin-off book during the frequent commercial breaks? Or are they seated there in a daze, like the TV-bound people of all ages in Chauncey Hare's *Interior America*? Only Clark Kent could tell, if he hasn't by now lost his super-powers for good. Mask is the key word. Yet the inscrutable Victorian-style white or yellow wood facades of several old houses look good, on their own terms, in summer and winter, when icicles and snow turn them into hastily constructed wedding cakes. Certain isolated details are especially good. You walk down the street, scanning it intently from left to right, and back again, striving to see what you can see, while you can.

Illustrations

A NOTE ON THE TYPE

The text of this book was set via computer-driven cathode-ray tube in Simoncini Garamond, a modern version by Francesco Simoncini of the type first cut by Claude Garamond (ca. 1490–1561). Garamond was a pupil of Geoffroy Tory and is believed to have based his letters on the Venetian models, although he introduced a number of important differences, and it is to him we owe the letter that we know as old-style. He gave to his letters a certain elegance and a feeling of movement that won for their creator an immediate reputation and the patronage of Francis I of France.

Composed by Centennial Graphics, Inc., Ephrata, Pennsylvania.

Printed by Coral Graphic Services, Long Island City, New York.

Bound by The Book Press, Brattleboro, Vermont

Designed by Judith Henry